D1728192

The Exchange

Shirley Woods

TRILOGY CHRISTIAN PUBLISHERS
TUSTIN, CA

The Exchange

Trilogy Christian Publishers
A Wholly Owned Subsidiary of Trinity Broadcasting Network
2442 Michelle Drive Tustin, CA 92780

Manufactured in the United States of America

10 9 8 7 6 5 4 3 2 1

Library of Congress Cataloging-in-Publication Data is available.

ISBN: 978-1-64773-876-1

E-ISBN: 978-1-64773-877-8

Adam and Eve Attempt to Cover Their Nakedness

And the eyes of them both were opened, and they knew that they were naked; and they sewed fig leaves together, and made themselves aprons. And they heard the voice of the LORD God walking in the garden in the cool of the day: and Adam and his wife hid themselves from the presence of the LORD God amongst the trees of the garden. And the LORD God called unto Adam, and said unto him, Where art thou? And he said, I heard thy voice in the garden, and I was afraid, because I was naked; and I hid myself. And he said, Who told thee that thou wast naked? Has thou eaten from the tree, whereof I commanded thee that thou shouldest not eat?

Genesis 3:7

Contents

Foreword

As a pastor, my life has revolved around the journey not only I'm on, but also around those who have been a part of my calling. One thing is certain, life is full of questions, hurts, problems and, for so many, defeat. The result that the defeated experience is the distorted belief that the God of love has forgotten their existence. Many wonder, does He care? Can anyone feel my pain? Will I ever be happy in this life?

In *The Exchange*, Shirley Woods takes you on her personal journey filled with heartache, questions, and brokenness. As a young, innocent child a battle began that very few could endure. Yet, in this work, she walks you through the simple understanding of how she allowed God to reveal to her His true identity. Because of Him, she has proven that anyone can overcome and truly experience life as a "happily ever after" experience. You will enjoy her transparency, hope in God, and the power to overcome. Enjoy the ride as you discover "The Exchange" God has for your life.

–Pastor Kelly Galati, Family Life Church, and friend.

Preface

God's intention for us all is to grow up in Paradise. Unfortunately, we live in a place subject to the limits of sin. At its best, it is the worst of Paradise.

LAYING A FOUNDATION

My formative years were spent in confusion. Many of my adult years were a continuation of that same confusion and emotional pain compounded by anger.

I was number eight of eleven children. As a toddler, I was initiated into a world I had no ability to deal with. I don't remember when it started, only that it ended when I turned eight due to the death of my oldest brother. He was eighteen when he died. I don't know much about his life, because he was thirteen years older. I know more about his death and the effects it had on my family.

The farthest thing from the mind of an eighteen-year-old, who has so much living yet to do, is the thought of death. My brother and his friends were out drinking. On the way home, the driver lost control of the vehicle and drove into a ditch. My brother was in the back seat (this was in the days before seat belts). The impact of the car hitting the ditch caused the back door to open. My brother was found with his head wedged between the frame of the car and the door. He lay in the hospital comatose for two weeks before he died. I believe in that time he reconciled his life with his Maker.

Because God is a loving and gracious Dad, He gives all His children equal opportunity to exchange their fig leaves for his righteous covering—the shed blood of His son, Jesus. To wish the wrath of God on my brother would be asking God to play favorites. Clearly, in His Word, He reveals that He is "no respecter of persons." He does not prefer one of His children over another. It took a while, but I know that now.

My hope is that God pursued my brother while fighting for life and moving toward death. To me, the coma was a state whereby the redemption of my brother's spirit was offered in exchange for the fig leaves of the flesh he had sewn in his short life. It was a time when the reality of his circumstances met with his fallen state, and he was given the opportunity to choose his fate.

God's will is that all men be saved. Forgiveness is the key to righteousness, peace, and joy in the Holy

Ghost—God's forgiveness offered to man through Jesus, and man's forgiveness of self and others. Because this is His will, I know He did whatever it took to create circumstances that allowed my brother a choice—the choice to exchange his fig leaves sewn in the flesh for salvation.

Understanding the facts about my early years allowed the windows of heaven to open. By exchanging those facts for God's truth, I was able to stop running and receive all the blessings I can hardly contain. This is the record of Love that never fails. The Exchange. It took place over a period of many years as God continued to pursue me where I was—always hoping, always expecting the best, and never keeping a record of the wrongs I had done. I was protected, provided for, and loved along the way. If it had happened any other way, my flesh could not have stood it.

CHAPTER 1

The Temptation

At first sight, when a baby is born, a declaration about that baby is made by the doctor and/or nurses in attendance: "It's a boy" or "it's a girl!" This is the identity of that child until death, unless there is an experience that touches them at the core of who they are. Sexual abuse is one of those experiences.

Introduction into sexual stimulus and activity requires more gray matter, with more connections, than a child possesses. Many times, it requires more than an adult possesses, especially when the circumstances are outside the boundaries of God's good intention. In his book, *Healing for Damaged Emotions*, David Seamands describes

> the introduction to sex as an obsession that can produce the deadliest of all emotional conflicts: dread and desire, fear and pleasure, love and hate, all combined into a violent, emotional earthquake which can tear a per-

son's guts out. All the way from childish curiosities, where children explore each other's bodies, to older brothers and sisters, with threats or bribes, taking advantage of younger ones and arousing powerful feelings. This is destructive at that age, like running 800 volts through 110 wire. Move on to fathers and stepfathers who treat their daughters or sons, not as daughters or sons, but as a wife or mistress" (1992, 127).

In his book, *The Wounded Heart*, Dan Allander describes shame as a "hemorrhage of the soul—an awful experience that makes us aware that we are seen as deficient and undesirable by someone who we hope will deeply enjoy us" (1973, 127). This was my experience. I was introduced to sex by my oldest brother, who had no more idea than I what responsibilities or consequences are connected to that experience. The result was an open portal for a demonic stronghold—shame.

As an adult, I found it difficult to sort through the trauma of that experience. In my heart, I knew the trauma of being victimized by one human being's will against another's. However, my mind continued to battle against the knowledge I had received of a Redeemer. How then, could I have understood the tangled web of confusion, created as a toddler, when the experiences of my past conflicted with the knowledge of God and His word?

Every child is born with three God-given needs to be met by parents and family: safety, significance, and unconditional love. At the age where these needs are unmet, or at the age where these needs are trumped by trauma, is the age and stage of life that a child remains emotionally stuck.

Chronologically, I got older. My body developed naturally, but my emotional state stagnated. As I aged, my spirit continued to cry for mercy as I chastised my flesh for its carnality, while at the mercy of its never-ending desires. I was emotionally retarded and spiritually ignorant. There was no obvious lack that could be detected by my parents, the authorities, or by my peers. Outwardly, I played hard and tough. I was respectful when necessary and very critical when my virtues were ignored. I was an okay student—not head of the class, but certainly not one of the "dumb" kids. Outwardly, I was aggressive and proud, refusing to let anyone get the best of me. While inwardly, I was a bowl of jello hoping that I would not have to defend the stand I always seemed to take against the "world."

As an adult, I recognized the act of the past that created the hemorrhage. As a child, it was nothing more than a promise to go to the school picnic or receive a nickel or a Tootsie Pop. In the mind of a child, the abuse was a means to an end. Although I didn't like it, unless I could avoid getting "caught," I didn't resist—I didn't know I could. As an adult, this was my way to rationalize and protect myself from the fear of being weak and preyed upon. This was a way of legalizing my shame and guilt, brought on by the rewards received for an unholy act. Even though I was a baby, I knew there was something 'just not right' about what happened to me. If I did believe that, why didn't I tell someone? Why didn't I resist?

In order to avoid the truth about "my sin," I focused on others. I focused on my mother. As far as I concerned, there was nothing worse than being weak, and I perceived my mother as weak. Weakness meant vulnerability and vulnerability meant abuse.

My mother suffered ridicule and criticism from my father for years. I determined, at a very early age, never to depend on anyone for any reason. What is interesting to me, now, is that I blamed my mother's abuse by my dad as the reason for my declaration of independence. Until now, although I knew my experience of victimization played a part in my decision-making process, I did not consider it the root cause of that declaration: never to be dependent. I looked outside myself for a scapegoat; my mother was an easy target. As I write, I am still receiving revelation (incredible—God is a God of detail!).

Today, I have greater understanding about what Linda, my ministry partner, used to say: "You can't always help what happens to you, but you can help what you do with what happens to you." In other words, I may have been a victim of someone else's bad choices, but the behaviors I developed to survive those experiences are my responsibility. My attitude and fears are my responsibility, also. Innocence created an open door for the enemy to kill, steal, and destroy my potential at a very early age. Fear closed the door, and shame kept me in the dark—hiding from the Truth.

You've heard it said before, and so have I: one sin is not more or less than another. That statement about sin didn't make any more sense to me early on than it does now to some of you. Jesus said, if you break the least part of the law, you break the whole law. Paul says that sins against the body carry a greater burden of guilt for the sinner. I believe it has to do with defiling what doesn't belong to us: our temples. Another reason may be that, in order to survive the defiling, we try to redefine the purpose of the temple not to house the image and likeness of God, but to satisfy our lusts. Sin is sin, and the damage it does to the soul and the body creates a kind of cave, or prison, of our own making.

In the mind of a child that needs to be tended to and kept safe, I was like a lamb led to the slaughter. As an adult, I know the Redeemer and His love that set me free, because He became my substitute lamb and was slaughtered on my behalf. As a child, I feared...as an adult, I met the keeper of the keys of righteousness, peace, and joy in the Holy Ghost.

CHAPTER 2

"If Only"

I attended an all-girls high school: The Academy of Notre Dame. Sounds prestigious, huh? The school no longer exists, but I am grateful for the experience of going to the same school my mother and sisters attended. While I participated in the painful process of a high school education, I certainly didn't care about it. Too much competition from too many girls, and I didn't have the energy to invest in what I knew I couldn't win at. Everyday I attended school, was a reminder that I didn't belong and that my investment would be rejected. So, when I go home at 3:30, I would lie down and sleep, so I didn't have to think about the day and failure of being me. Sometimes, I would get up for a few minutes to eat, and sometimes I would sleep straight through to morning. When morning came, and it was time to get up for school, I could hardly make it as I felt the exhaustion of "waiting" for the day life would take on meaning and I would have purpose. My hope was that when I graduated, I would find the satisfaction I was looking for. *If only* I could do hair and start making my own money. *If only* I could do what I always dreamed about; then I would be happy. I would feel good about me. I will have arrived!

For whatever reason, my dad paid for my cosmetology education after graduation. My dad was not one to do something for nothing, and I braced myself against his expectations of owning his own business through me. When I graduated, I would pay him back as soon as I got a job—his idea not mine. Then, he would set me up in a shop. I secretly rejected that idea immediately, not wanting to be indebted to the man I hated.

Not until I took my state exam, and had my license in hand, did I reveal the awkward truth that I was not interested in his proposition. My dad accepted it exactly the way you would imagine. He demanded his pound of flesh and settled for a lifetime of grooming. UUUGH!

As I was still living at home during my education, it was difficult for me to avoid his demands—hard as I tried. Before I graduated beauty school, I was offered a job at a salon that served a wealthier clientele. In no time at all, I was making pretty good money. Before I knew it, I was moving out— finally! It wasn't difficult for me to stay away for longer periods of time. *If only* I could break the family ties that bound me; I would be free!

I did well in beauty school. At least, I did well academically and creatively. Socially, I was a failure. So much so that one of my instructors took notice. She was very diplomatic and kind. Even then, I figure she saw something in me no one else could, or maybe no one else wanted to. It was difficult to see the me held captive by a very thick, high wall of guilt and shame that came with attitude.

She brought to me a life-changing book to read that she said may be the difference between hair working for my success or me working to be a success at doing hair. The name of the book was *How to Win Friends and Influence People* by Dale Carnegie. Even then, God was using others to bring me to Him. Miss Charlene was a willing vessel that took on the challenge.

What I learned was that not everyone has to be my friend and, if they didn't like me (I couldn't even imagine it), I could still practice my creative talents on their heads and collect a fee. What a concept! Unfortunately, I didn't understand the wisdom of that book until much later. Nevertheless, I thanked Miss Charlene and decided that she must like me, because she took the time to give me something. I spent the rest of my time in beauty school trying to repay her kindness. I made a pest of myself. There was nothing she could ask that I wouldn't offer to do. Sometimes, I wasn't chosen for the job, and I interpreted it as rejection. I was devastated, but she remained consistently kind, reminding me that every-one needed an opportunity to participate. In my mind, I was the only one that mattered—*I had to be*. After all, she gave me a gift. (Remember, a favor for a gift—the school picnic, a nickel, or a Tootsie Pop)? The means to an end? The unconscious example becomes a pattern to be repeated without thought. Miss Charlene took no-tice and did something for me, now it was up to me to repay the favor if it took a thousand different ways to do it. Then, if enough favors were done, she would owe me again, and on, and on...until each relationship be-comes a manipulative power struggle.

Regardless of my distorted thinking, some people are genuinely good and desire to help others. She was one of those people, so she didn't fall for my manipula-tive tactics. I didn't need to buy her attention, nor did she ever stop revealing hard truth to me.

I graduated beauty school on time. I passed my state board with flying colors. Not because of manipulation and control, but because I worked hard and didn't allow anything to distract me from the goal. My mother went with me to Springfield as my model and my compan-ion. True to my nature, I was ungrateful. Mother was a trooper.

I had a job before I graduated from beauty school. Glenda had three shops she needed to fill and regularly called the school for new recruits. On the Tuesday I got home from Springfield, I began work at Snooty Fox Salon. I thought I was everyone's answer for perfection. As I watched and worked, I found out differently.

I walked in the door and recognized a girl that went to high school with my sister's boyfriend. The first words that came out of my mouth sounded like an accusation about her and Carl. She went to high school with him and they spent a lot of time working together on floats and banners and school functions. She had a boyfriend of her own and, although she liked Carl, she wasn't interested in dating him. Thankfully, she was not as defensive as I was and was able to overlook that remark. Later, as Yvonne and I developed a strong friendship, she laughed about that experience saying, "that was the dumbest thing I ever heard anyone say as an opening statement." I wasn't surprised. I got used to the taste of my foot a long time ago. Carol was another of the girls that I worked with. She annoyed me with her cute little smile and great figure. She was always happy, and that made me jealous. Meg was quiet and creative. Every day I was in competition with her creativity which I could not match. That annoyed me too. Everything and everybody annoyed me—I annoyed me! Meg probably didn't know we were in competition, but secretly I compared and competed with everyone, because everyone was better, and more creative, more liked, skinnier, or cuter than me.

I was intimidated by Bonnie, who seemed to know everything there was to know about life and hair. She was divorced with a baby girl. She seemed to be in control of her life and have everything going for her. I secretly decided that she was my new hero and set out to be just like her. Although I still greatly admire her, she was nonetheless just as human as me, much to my surprise. But then, my perception was my reality, and I didn't know how I was going to compete with my new fellow employees when I had nothing to offer but my shame-based self, full of inadequacies—no doubt lower than the standard of those I would be associated with in a profession that promoted perfection.

On the upside, I was doing what I knew was the **key** to my happiness, and I was looking forward to a new beginning!

CHAPTER 3

What Was I Thinking?

Carol and Clem were my very dearest friends. They were old enough to be my parents. They didn't have children of their own, and I was glad to fill their void by playing the part of their daughter. That's probably why I was so attracted to them. They gave me what I needed—**all** the attention! And until Clem died, I called him Father.

Carol never had any children. Clem had one daughter from a previous marriage, but she lived with her mom in another state. I did Carol's hair every Saturday and came to visit Clem at least once a week, unless he needed his hair cut. Clem's father was a barber so, of course, Clem was an "expert." Not only was he an expert, he was more than willing to offer me the benefit of his wisdom like any dad would do for their child. And so, I learned how to manipulate a comb and scissor like a barber to get a neat neckline. Carol was our willing model.

I would go to their house any night of the week, and especially on weekends. Bill (my husband) was not usually with me. During the week, we would sit and watch TV until the news was over, and then I would go home. On weekends, we would spend time on the patio or visiting the neighbors who rented from Clem and Carol and had become friends. Sometimes we played Bingo during the week—the three of us.

One of their neighbors, Dee, later became a client and a pretty good friend. We shared stories about living with men who didn't seem to like us, since they always had an excuse for leaving us behind. We both liked playing Bingo, and we both got what we needed from our good friend Carol. Dee was quite a bit older than me, so I didn't feel she was much competition when it came to Carol and Clem's time and attention. My position in the "family" was safe.

For a long time, we three couples were inseparable. Every holiday there seemed to be a dinner dance to attend. Special events connected to political contributions and connections, as well as retirement dinners and dances. We brought in many New Years together and celebrated the births of children and grandchildren. Then Clem retired from working for one of the local concrete companies. How unfair, that shortly after his retirement, he was stricken with cancer.

My heart was sick. The concern for my pain became greater than the last months of comfort I could have offered to my passing hero. I visited off and on, but felt my presence would have been too bothersome and difficult for Clem—especially since I now had two children that seemed to be attached to my hips. I was not available on the day he died, but occasionally

I did go to him. He knew who I was and forever encouraged me to return. Carol continued to work while Clem was sick. She didn't retire until she had heart surgery and was required to change her lifestyle and manage her stress level.

After the birth of my second child, it became too complicated to spend time together. I stopped working at the salon. For a while, Carol came to my house or I went to hers. Then, one day, she decided that our arrangement was getting too complicated as my time and energy was exhausted with three children. Carol made a standing appointment at a shop that was closer to home and more convenient. Our friendship slowly dwindled after that. I send a Christmas card every year and thank her for her match-making ability. Last year, I received an unexpected phone call from her. She is retired and well.

Carol and Clem were people I loved, and I believe God used them in my redemption because they were available to be used. That part of my life is a treasure chest of good examples of how a wife should treat her husband and how a husband should love his wife. They were also good for my esteem, as they contributed to my feeling safe, significant, and unconditionally loved. Had it not been for Carol, I would not have even met my husband.

Bill worked with Carol at the phone company. After we married, he didn't spend as much time with them outside of work as I did. His life was consumed by his first love—the Army Reserves. I was satisfied living in my fantasy world with Clem and Carol as my "parents," working and making money doing what I believed was my destiny. As long as I could go to Carol and Clem's house when I wanted, and use my money for what I desired, my fantasy remained intact. Not because Bill was horrible did I feel this way, but he disturbed my fantasy. He had the nerve to ask for time, energy, and attention I *"couldn't"* give. In my world, I was the center of the universe, and I didn't have to "share my square with anyone."

The first time I met Bill, I felt I had met the man of my dreams. I had never dated. What did I know about the man of my dreams? He was a blind date—a set up through my client who worked with him. He was recently divorced, had one child, and was in the Army Reserves. That's about all Carol could tell me. There's a number of reasons why people who date without knowing each other are referred to as blind. I probably fit them all!

I was enamored by this man I didn't know. Bill was recently divorced when Carol asked if I was interested in going out with him. I wasn't dating at the time (I had never dated until that time) and didn't figure I had anything to lose.

He showed up promptly at 6:00 p.m.—his 6'2" frame filled my door, and he smiled as though he had a secret. Bill's style is a starched button-down shirt with a pair of kaki chinos and loafers. To this day, it remains his signature style. His blonde hair and hazel eyes captured my soul. I was smitten. I can't remember what we said by way of introduction, something stupid I'm sure. I only remember grabbing my purse, getting in the car, and heading toward St. Louis to the "Hill"—an exclusive area of Italian restaurants. Unfortunately, the restaurant we chose was closed for vacation. It must not have occurred to us to try another in the area. There were many to choose from. All of them serving the finest Italian cuisine, hence the area being named "The Hill." We simply headed back toward home to eat at a local Ground Round. (That pretty much sums up our modus operandi for the rest of our lives). If plan "A" doesn't work out, get frustrated and head towards home.

By then, I was starving and unable to carry on much of a conversation. Bill's stomach tends to rule him and, for the next 30 miles, we were quiet. He was unable to focus on anything but his growling stomach, and I felt better being quiet than risk saying something stupid— I was sure I had done enough of that already. We both smoked early in our relationship, and that night we must have each smoked a pack on the way back from the Hill, a forty five minute ride.

Since the restaurant was closed, Bill asked if I was interested in stopping at White Castle to hold us over. Unfortunately for Bill, I didn't even know what a White Castle was. Not wanting to appear uninformed, I declined. Fortunately for me, a White Castle burger is a favorite of Bill's, and it wasn't long before I became acquainted with them. (If I had known then what I found out later, we would have stopped and filled up on those luscious little patties of soy and beef on tiny buns.)

I met Bill in June. Aside from a major bump in the road in the middle of our relationship (Bill decided he wanted to break up with me for reasons I will explain later) our time together was pretty easy. We met in June, and we married on the 27th of December. My mom and dad, Bill's mom and dad, and the judge were in attendance. On a chilly afternoon, standing in the living room of my efficiency apartment, we said "I do—until death us do part."

God is a **big** God. I didn't know how big until now.

I would have liked to have a big wedding, but Bill insisted it was not a good idea, because he had already been married and anyone who was anyone had already given their gifts the first time around. There was no big wedding the first time, and it wasn't like family and friends had the opportunity to share in the joy of the moment, but Bill's mom told him it would be inappropriate to make announcements. Also, what was never made clear was the short amount of time between getting married, getting divorced, and our dating. I didn't bother to find out, and Bill never divulged.

I was so in love with the idea of being in love. Surely, this would be the end of my struggle to be someone! This was the missing piece in my fantasy plan. When my wish came true, and he proposed, I wasn't even sure it happened. The circumstances were so strange, I had to ask Bill his intention by rephrasing the statement as a question: "Did you just ask me to marry you?" The experience was less than what I expected, but I reassured myself that it was a minor glitch. It was my fantasy, and I could rewrite the script to make it appear more romantic.

My *fantasy* went something like this: The man of my dreams would come into my life, sweep me off my feet, and whisk me away into a blissful existence where our love sustained us. We would take long drives through the countryside, basking in the moment with nothing to distract us but the wind in our faces. Much like Audrey Hepburn and Cary Grant, Grace Kelly and Cary Grant—*anybody* and Cary Grant. The moment when my fantasy collided with reality, we were driving down Main Street on our way home from a good meal and a movie. (This time we played it safe and stayed in town to eat.)

That night, we saw the movie *Solient Green*. Charleton Heston is featured as a futuristic law enforcer, and Edward G. Robinson plays the part of his father. It's the story of a concrete jungle, void of vegetation and the ability to sustain human life as natural elements were used up. Morality was questionable and ethics were based on the ability to deceive. The movie revolves around this product used to provide nutrition, as there was no other means for sustaining life. Charleton Heston discovers the truth about this product when his father signs his life away for one last view of how the world used to be. The final statement, made at the end of the movie by Charleton Heston after his father died, was, "Solient green is people!" This was not a feel-good, romantic film starring Cary Grant. It certainly didn't set the stage for a proposal. But that didn't stop my practical husband, who had his mind made up.

We were almost home, and Bill began discussing tax time. He casually mentioned the deductions he would have this year as opposed to last year. Then, nonchalantly, he asked if I would like to become one of his permanent deductions. I was not quite sure what he was asking, so I restated it. Did you just ask me to marry you? He didn't pull over; he didn't slow down. He just looked over at me, smiled, and said, "That's right, are you interested?" I didn't think about it. I didn't hesitate. I looked over at him, smiled, and said, "Yes."

Finally, I could be somebody! Finally, I would have an identity that was not connected to shame!

We married two weeks after the proposal. On December 27th—the same day his mom and dad celebrated their marriage, we were married in my apartment by his friend, Steve. He was a judge Bill knew through the Army Reserves. The night of our wedding, we went to our favorite dive and did what we always did: escape from who we were to the best of our ability with the aid of alcohol. The only difference was, the money that bought our escape this time came from all those who refused to believe we were just like them. Instead, they toasted and celebrated what they still had hope in—a new beginning and a different end than the one they themselves experienced. Bill and I projected the ideal couple with absolute regard for one another. We were the epitome of fresh, new love that was destined to last a lifetime.

Unfortunately, the end of our fantasy came faster than the beginning, or so it felt like to me. My world came crashing down the second day of marriage. Our first night was the way you might expect from two young people blinded by their hopes, and dreams, and lots of alcohol. The next day was another story. I was determined to recreate the wedding night of my dreams, so the next night, after some Kentucky Fried Chicken with all the fixins, I changed into something 'wedding night-ish' while my husband changed into something that was wedding nightmarish. He had become angry about my alcohol consumption, my behavior, the food, the apartment, and negligee I bought and stored for this special night. (My whole life I planned for my salvation from shame. When I was a senior in high school, I bought this negligee while on a shopping spree. I was sure that my future husband would see me in this and fall hopelessly in love with me, thanking God that I was his. I stored it carefully, anticipating the day when my dreams would become reality.)

I cried for a while as I lay with my back turned away from him. Of course, he couldn't imagine what was wrong. According to him, he was just telling me how he felt. After all, weren't we supposed to be open and honest with each other? By morning, I decided to put this behind me like Scarlett when she stood in the middle of desecration and devastation, fists raging against an unseen force, declaring, "If I think about this now, I'll go crazy." I started a new file marked "marriage." I put another brick on my wall of protection and planned for an alternative to happiness.

In *Healing for Damaged Emotions*, David Seamands compares a marriage between two people with unlimited needs to two ticks and no dog:

> Many married people fail to allow God to do for them what only God can do. Then they ask other human beings, their spouses, to what they cannot possible do. If they worked at it, men make good husbands, and women make good wives. But they make lousy gods. They're not meant for that. And all those wonderful promises that people make o their wedding day--'I promise to love, care for you, cherish you, through all the circumstances and vicissitudes of life'--these are possible only when a heart is secure in God's love, grace, and care. Only a forgiven and graced soul can keep such promises. What the person often really means when he says those beautiful words is, 'I have a lot of terrific inner needs and inner emptiness and debts to pay and I'm going to

give you a marvelous opportunity to fill my Grand Canyon and take care of me, Aren't I wonderful? This behavior is compared to a tick on a dog. The tick isn't really interested in a good life for the dog; he's simply taking all the time. The tragedy with some marriages is that both partners are takers, and the marriage is like two ticks and no dog! Two collectors and nothing to collect (1992, 49).

Bill and I were the two ticks in search of prey.

I didn't talk to Bill for almost one week after that incident, except when I had to. It's not in Bill's nature to investigate the feelings of another. That might mean he would have to compromise or create a solution to heal the relationship. Maybe he would have to take some responsibility for the problem, which would create another problem. Instead, he would intimidate to get his needs met. He had his tactics and I had mine—something I figured out at a very early age. Seething in silence, glaring with eyes of fire, is my response to intimidation. When necessary, I would spout words that dripped with venom if he asked for more than I was willing to give. He knew I was mad, and he walked on eggshells around me for a while. Served him right. He would suffer silently and have enough of my anger, which gave him a good reason to spend more time at the Reserve Center or sleep on the couch. Then I would begin to feel lonely and need to find a way to resolve this without giving in. I resorted to familiar patterns of thinking or "old tapes" about blaming, and denying, and problem-solving—even though they never worked, even though those old tapes often created more drama and greater consequence. I didn't know that then, but it was the best I could do.

The dialogue in my head went something like this,

Maybe you misunderstood Bill. He wouldn't hurt you, he pledged to love and cherish you.

No, I didn't misunderstand.

Bill is mean.

Don't be stupid.

What were you thinking? What did you expect?

It must be my fault, I was the one who caused him to get mad.

He doesn't have a problem, I do.

I can't believe it.

He's a creep, and I hate him!

He should appreciate what I did for him.

I must have misunderstood.

No, he's the one who doesn't appreciate what I tried to do for him.

I tried too hard.

He doesn't need me.

I better do something to make everything alright.

He might get mad at me forever!

It couldn't be my fault.

I couldn't be the mistake.

There must be something else. There has to be something else.

It wasn't my fault, he must know something.

He knows...How could he know? I didn't tell him. Who told him?

How can he be this way?

It's the way men are.

Stay ahead of him. Don't be weak!

He's the best thing that ever happened to me. I better make this right before I lose him forever.

In the mind of a codependent woman, identified by shame and guilt of past experiences, making mistakes becomes a shameful experience that is familiar. In the mind of the codependent, the solution is not to take responsibility and deal with the issues but hide from them. The issues that created the problem are ignored or denied. Therefore, the problem is interpreted as a lack on the part of the other person in the relationship and not the shame and guilt that identifies the codependent who needs to be needed. The solution becomes the need to live above the pain of what she knows about herself and cannot escape. The problem is suppressing the past or hiding from the past, while living in the present and recreating the new identity. When there is a possibility that the codependent may be discovered, they often look to someone or something else to blame for all that goes wrong in life.

All of this is hindsight of course. The problem is really facing the truth about past experiences. The problem is confusion, which feels like weakness and vulnerability. The solution is to expose, acknowledge, and forgive self and others. The solution is to sort out the experience by taking and giving responsibility for choices and acknowledge the behaviors created to survive, rather than trust God.

I was too full of pride to **admit** anything could be wrong with me. I would throw Bill under the bus before I would admit my flaws. Nonetheless, I had to find a solution for an unnamed dilemma, and it wasn't going to be logical according to those who think rationally. To me, it was genius!

CHAPTER 4

Maybe This...

Eventually, we began to talk. We had to; my apartment was too little to avoid each other. It was just a two-room efficiency with a closet-kitchen and one bathroom. In any room I could carry on a conversation using my inside voice, talk through walls, and be heard as easily as if I were standing next to the person I was addressing. Actually, I lived in a four-plex that afforded me the comfort of knowing I wasn't alone without having to share my space with the other three tenants. So, in order to avoid the pitfalls of my parents and my siblings, who all married low-life losers, (according to me) we had to come to some kind of amicable arrangement. I had something to prove (being better than...) and something to hide (shame of my past). The cost of arguing any longer was too high, and I determined to live the fantasy "happily ever after." So, I sucked it up and I took the blame for "that one," as I vowed to my husband to be a better wife. Most of all, I told myself that taking the blame made me strong and not weak. Taking the blame made me the bigger person.

And then I convinced myself that I was the one who presumed to know Bill's likes and dislikes without asking. It was I who assumed his love for me would separate me from my shame and carry me into the blissful arms of acceptance. I made an ass out of him and me. I needed to fix it.

Or perhaps there was another solution to the dilemma I had created. Maybe I didn't create this dilemma, but something was wrong with my knight in shining armor? What if it wasn't my lack of understanding or the yellow nightie—which, by the way, I got rid of. What if Bill is just a creep? No, he's perfect. (He had to be for my redemption to take place.) If he is perfect, then it must be something on the outside influencing him to be so unhappy. He talked about his son an awful lot. What if he was missing his son? What if the burden of his divorce and loss of his son had created a void which made him sad? Maybe there was no other way for him to express his sadness except to get mad at me. This was feeling like the truth more and more. There was much to think about. (Did I tell you I had a great sense for predicting the future? It's a gift all codependents possess and a requirement for those of us who have control issues.)

Surely, encouraging my husband to fight for his child would convince him I had his best interest at heart. This would be my redemption in his eyes and in the eyes of my in-laws. Bill would believe I was once again worthy of being his wife.

Bill's son, Billy, spent a great deal of time with us when we dated. After the first few times we went out, our dates revolved around him and going places that were entertaining and kid friendly. That should have been a red flag, but "love is blind." Truthfully, the need to be needed is far-sighted, and I rejected the reality glasses that would allow me to clearly see my present situation.

Right now, I could think of only one thing: redeeming myself. What I didn't know then was that my best intention for Bill and his son couldn't make up for his guilt or make him happy. I was so emotionally stunted that I couldn't see happiness isn't a destiny, but a journey. Getting custody of Billy was not the answer to "Happily Ever After." If someone had told me, I would not have listened, since I always knew better than anyone. To listen, you had to trust, and I made up my mind at an early age that was never going to happen.

As it turned out, Billy coming to live with us was another tragedy of errors for Billy and us. I wasn't ready for the responsibility required for childcare. I used to baby sit, but before I really got sick of the kids, the parents came home, and I left. There was no getting away from the responsibility of this kid, and I was getting tired. My plan to make Bill happy backfired. Instead of making him happy, the care and feeding of his child gave him the excuse he needed to spend time with his first love, the Army.

Bill almost seemed happy for a while. He was even smiling and hanging out at home more. All was right with the world, like when a baby is born and life takes on new meaning. After a while, the newness wore off. Phone calls started coming from the guys at the Reserve Center who missed him. Bill began to make excuses for leaving, telling me we needed the extra money he made by going to meetings. This didn't make sense to me since we weren't paying child support anymore. I said I understood and sent him on his way with a kiss. I was a fool in love and didn't recognize what was happening. For a while, I was the good wife and mother, but all the time, energy, and money we spent on getting custody of Bill's son wasn't making Bill happy anymore, and now I was getting unhappy too. Just because you want something doesn't mean you should have it. And just because you need to be liked and/or loved doesn't mean you will be— especially by a child living in the middle of two worlds.

Children of divorce live in the father's world, and the mother's world, and belong to neither and to both.

For the most part, Billy and I spent our time competing for the attention of someone who never noticed either of us. Unfortunately, I was much older and, therefore, should have been wiser. Too bad I didn't know that when he first came to live with us.

*******Guilt is a nonproductive motivator. Guilt is never satisfied with accomplishing a "resolution." The purpose of guilt is to keep its target in turmoil, not to get positive results or find a solution. Guilt is a tactic of the enemy that produces condemnation and torment. Condemnation is a negative force that focuses on the problem. Condemnation focuses on what "woulda," "coulda," "shoulda" been done and how bad you are for not doing it. Negative thoughts produce negativity and more guilt. Guilt always multiplies itself and becomes overwhelming. Guilt always needs an outlet. Mine was anger—for now.*

*To find solution, the Holy Spirit brings conviction. Conviction brings with it creativity. It is a positive tool that focuses on a solution benefiting everyone involved. The end result is redemption.**************

Romans 8:1 says, "There is therefore now no condemnation to those who are in Christ Jesus."

What an absolutely wonderful revelation! No condemnation, no guilt, no need for an outlet.

I was always angry, and now Billy knew it too! Not only was I ashamed and guilty, but I added to my cache of identities: being a martyr. How wonderful I was to take in Bill's son and raise him. What a great sacrifice I was making on his behalf. I must be a saint!

That's not what Billy thought. Billy knew we hadn't known each other when his parents were married, so I couldn't have been the reason they broke up. However, as far as he was concerned, I was the reason his mom and dad couldn't get back together. He didn't feel one way or the other about me as an individual, and certainly not as a mother figure. There was no way he was going to call me mom, making that clear from the beginning. Most of the time, my feelings got in the way of being the rational authority. There were a few times we were able to call a truce, like when we went to the in-laws. For the rest of our time together, we silently battled for what neither of us could possess—Bill. Both of us hurting. Both of us blaming the other for our pain.

***********_There are so many children born without benefit of both parents in a loving relationship, committed through marriage and blessed by God. When children are born within the parameters of marriage and their needs for safety, significance, and unconditional love are unmet, they too gather stones along the way. Emotional rocks are stored in an unseen bag that burdens the spirit, soul, and body of the person carrying it. Those who bond with the hurting become targets for unleashing the pain that was caused by neglect and abuse. The emotional rocks keep others at a distance by hurting them or creating a "barrier" around the heart of_ *the hurting. Rocks are gathered and stored to use on anyone and everyone for all that has gone wrong and all that is wrong presently. It is a lose/lose situation for everyone involved—especially children.*

Along with the child or children of a previous relationship, often comes an ex with no established boundaries of communication and contact. Unless boundaries are created, a whole bunch of unmet needs and unresolved issues create distractions and questions for the new spouse. ***

Sometimes it felt like Bill was spending more time with his ex-wife on the phone or in the car dropping off and picking up his son than with me. Of course, I was jealous and hurt. No wonder God hates divorce. Had I known then what I know now, I don't think I would have gotten mixed up with Bill. Too late!

Because I know now what I didn't know then, I'm thankful to God that I got mixed up with Bill and that God is a God of restoration and redemption.

********When God declares His position about relationships, especially marriage, He has already made provision for a solution. Except for the hardened hearts of His children, there is no reason for the separation of what He joins together. If we humble ourselves and release control, He will redeem what Satan means to destroy.**********

This is the thinking of a rational person who understands God's love, protection, and provision. However, I was not rational. In fact, not only was I emotionally stunted, but spiritually stunted as well. That's why I believed that a child of my own would bring the desired effect I was looking for in my life and my marriage. I decided a child of our own would be the answer to the interference and distractions from my stepson's mother. I decided that, to gain all of Bill's attention, I would have to fight fire with fire. I was determined to win a battle with the "enemy." (Unfortunately, I didn't really know who the enemy was.) I had discovered the solution to all my problems! When I have a child born out of "our" love, it would create a stronger bond between me and Bill. This was probably the solution I had been looking for, and it would give me an identity that I was lacking in my present state...Maybe this would be the answer to my prayers. So far, nothing else had met my expectations to feel safe, find significance, and know that I was unconditionally loved. Certainly, a child from my body and our union would make the difference. I had new reason to hope.

It took a little longer than I wanted it too and required a few more doctor visits than I expected but, four years after we married, I was pregnant with our first child—*my* first child—*my* redemption!

The pregnancy was a little more difficult than I anticipated. I spent most of the first three months cuddled up to the toilet. As soon as the morning sickness began to dissipate, I developed a urinary tract infection that required hospitalization. After the first 5 months, the rest of the pregnancy was textbook perfect. I felt better than I had for a long time. I was getting a lot of attention from my family and friends, and I could eat all the watermelon and potato salad I wanted.

Nine months later, and exactly on the due date, Sarah, princess, took my breath away! There was no doubt in my mind that God had visited me with a gift that would be my solace, my identity, my new beginning. I was so proud of her! It was like having my own little baby doll (something else I never had growing up). I loved dressing her up, giving her a bath, feeding her, looking at her...I couldn't get enough of her. It wasn't long before I thought if one baby was this easy, imagine what two would be like.

Besides, she was so good for my self-esteem. I didn't go anywhere that someone wasn't telling me how cute she was and how good she was. If one baby brought that much attention, I imagined I would be the center of the universe having another.

A little longer than two years later, I was pregnant again. After the first month, when I thought I had the flu, I never got sick again until the end of my pregnancy. Then, the expansion of my belly created a lot of pressure on my stomach and the McChickens and strawberry shakes I ate everyday didn't sit so well. Nonetheless, I felt better than I could ever imagine. Pregnancy agreed with me.

When I started having my babies, there was no ultrasound so we played a guessing game as to which sex we would have. We picked out two names: Edward Arthur and Mary Kathryn. Secretly, I prayed for a Mary Kathryn, believing that God would not create through me the species that wreaked havoc in my life. I still did not trust males and couldn't imagine having to raise one. Bill wanted a boy, but I hoped God liked me better and would give me what I wanted. All of our children are named after an ancestor from one or both of our families. Bill's grandmother's name was Mary, and there was also a Kathryn that was Bill's great aunt. Regardless of what we put on the birth certificate, I intended to call her Katie.

What Bill didn't know, was that her name was chosen long before she was born. All through grade school, I had two best friends: Patty Richardson and Katie Guest. Patty spent a lot of time mad at me, so Katie and I hung out quite a bit. My friend, Katie, was a gorgeous redhead with green eyes who seemed to know how to have a good time. I spent a lot of nights and weekends at her house. I felt safe with her. Fortunately, there was a Mary Kathryn ancestor, since it was my intention to honor the memory of my friend by naming my daughter Katie. And most importantly, God loved me the best!

How coincidental that the names of my first two children happen to be the names I had chosen when I was declaring that I would never have children, because I didn't like them. By the way, that became my mantra when I first began working at Snooty Fox. It's one of Bonnie's favorite stories to tell when we get together. Considering that I birthed four children and raised five, it *is* pretty funny. And she gets a kick out of telling it.

Katie was my angel. So fair, she glowed with a halo of hair that remained almost undetectable for the first two years of her life. I was never happier. After the first week of feeling accomplished, the tears came. I didn't know what postpartum blues were until I experienced them. Even then, I wasn't sure of what was happening to me. Bill had little patience for what he considered my way of getting attention and neglecting him. So, regardless of what I was experiencing, there were two babies and Billy to take care of, and I didn't have time for any "nonsense."

Unfortunately, postpartum depression is not non-sense and, when recognized and treated, it allows a woman to heal faster. The bonding process between baby and mother is much more successful also. So much heart ache could have been avoided. I got so busy trying to feel normal that I ignored what made me feel strong: being needed by my babies. At that time, I don't know what I would have done without my sister, Carol. She loved my babies as much as I did and would spend almost every day with me. When she wasn't at my house, I was at her house, and I was constantly busy. Doing something kept me from being crazy and feeling depressed.

I'm sorry to say, my Katie suffered more than Sarah, who's bond with me was strong and viable due to different circumstances. I wasn't mean to my little Kate. She was beautiful and so easy! I breast fed her as I did Sarah. I changed her diaper, I bathed her, and talked to her. I loved her, but at a distance. I knew something was different, but I didn't discover what it was until much later when I was in school studying the effects of pregnancy and postpartum depression. Bonding is a significant part of mothering. The bonding process was postponed for almost a year after Katie's birth, as I struggled to regain control of my mind and emotions.

Two years after Mary Kathryn was born, despite birth control measures, I discovered I was pregnant again. It didn't take long for my hormones to multiply, and I was on top of the world. Still not sure if I was ready for another boy, we chose boy names and girl names, but silently I prayed for another girl. God answered my prayer. The universe and I were in harmony. Margaret Anne, named after my mother, was born on my sister's birthday. She was gorgeous!

Every baby born to me was another success story. I was beginning to think I could make birthing babies a life-time career. Surrogate mothers were not recognized then—a good thing, because I loved being pregnant. Unfortunately, the birth brought with it a mental madness that threatened to destroy me. It took almost a year before I could reclaim my emotions. When I was pregnant, my hormones were at a level that allowed me to think clearly and participate in life with a pretty decent attitude. While pregnant, we enjoyed a clean house, a clean car, and supper on the table every night when Bill got home. It was nothing for me to invest in hobbies and extra activities with enough energy left to complete the day as a loving caregiver for my children and husband. I sewed new soft sculptures for the baby's room, made a matching quilt, diaper caddy, and bumper pads. No one was without a hand-made gift for all the holidays. I made life size dolls to surprise my older girls when they came to visit their new "sister" for the first time at the hospital. There was nothing I couldn't do. I was invincible! That is until the baby was born, and my hormones crashed—again.

If I wasn't forced to go home after 4 days, I think I would still be in the hospital hiding from life. Something was definitely wrong, but I didn't have time to think about it. There was a house to clean, laundry to wash, babies to feed, and a husband to care for. So, I did what I did best; I created a fantasy world where I was perfect, I had enough sleep, and my husband thought I walked on water. Thank you, God for my sisters who took up my slack when it came to watching the kids. Not only was I not perfect in caring for the children, but I fell behind doing laundry and sometimes yard work. My house got cleaned because I would work myself into a frenzy over something stupid and need to use up the adrenaline before I released it on my family. (Funny, just the other day, my daughter asked me if I still yelled when I did housework).

The greater the crisis, the cleaner the house. By the time I was ready to put away my cleaning supplies, I had calmed down and could be civil toward the family again. Unfortunately, I created a monster "elephant" in the living room while cleaning. No one dared acknowledge it for fear it would be real and trample their little bodies. On some level, it had already damaged their souls and threatened to devour their spirits.

Innocent children that experience anger released on them learn early to flee the premises, waiting for the fire to die. During the cleaning frenzy, the family knew better than to distract me. They walked on eggshells for a while until the guilt of that frenzied experience got the best of me and I would take them to McDonald's, or the movies, or something that could say, "I'm sorry." God's grace is unlimited and was accessed a great deal on my kid's behalf when they were young. It didn't stop when they were older, as I was able to tell them about the experiences they had that were unacceptable, and then ask them for their forgiveness.

CHAPTER 5

From the Dead

I will digress a little here to help you understand God's love that pursues us and chases us down, manifesting at times when we least expect it.

This is the beginning of God's intervention to reclaim me and the end result when I surrendered. Although it began a few years after I was married, the surrendering took a little longer—six years longer.

At the time when I graduated beauty school, working in a salon was a different experience than it is now. We worked for a shop owner and were paid 55% commission. We were not required to purchase any supplies or towels, nor were we required to launder our own towels, as is often the case now. Our priority was to make money for the owner. One Tuesday evening, I was at the shop by myself. I had a late-night appointment—someone new to the shop. No one else wanted to stay late. We were "encouraged" not to reject any new clients. I was the newest hire and lowest in seniority.

It was up to me to stay and satisfy my obligation to my employer.

Anyway, after a shampoo, I began to cut, and she began to talk—about God. The first rule of cosmetology is never talk about politics or religion with your clients. We were alone, so it wasn't like anyone would know I had participated in breaking the rules. Nonetheless, I remember feeling very uncomfortable. Besides that, her perception of God conflicted with my own. As hard as I tried, I couldn't get her to change the subject.

I had been raised as a good Catholic girl to believe that my salvation was up to my ability to be good enough. Unfortunately, I knew I was never going to be good enough and rejected her best efforts to open the door for Jesus, who could make me good enough. I qualified my lack of interest to being Catholic. All I needed to know about God I learned in parochial schools, and I felt He and I had an understanding that didn't involve talking in public about Him. (How many times have you heard someone say they prefer to keep their faith private, because they have an understanding between themselves and "The Man Upstairs?" That's always a red flag for me today. It's the same excuse I used to ward off anyone bold enough to offer me understanding.) She was bold alright, and my discomfort about those things I didn't understand wasn't enough to keep her in check.

The tone of her voice, so much sincerity, and the passion with which she spoke influenced me more than her words. Then, she offered to pray for me. **What?!** I just dismissed all her best efforts to convince me of my need for a Savior and she wants to pray for me? She was persistent, and I was ready to get rid of her, so I agreed. No one was in the shop to witness, and I convinced myself that there was no harm in praying. I don't even remember if I gave her a good haircut. I never saw her again. I can't remember her name or really what she looked like, except for having long, golden-brown hair. Who knows, she may have been an angel. It was the first but wouldn't be the last time I had an encounter with them. There were two other occasions when I believe an angel was present on my behalf. *******One time, after salvation, my husband and I were hopelessly lost in an unknown area of Missouri and received directions from a stranger. We were stopped along the side of the road looking at the map when an older gentleman approached the window to ask my husband if we were lost. It seemed like the most natural thing to do. We were unafraid and very grateful. After giving us directions, he returned to his royal blue Pinto. As we drove away, I looked back and he was gone.*

The other time, I was traveling across a bridge while it was snowing. I was coming home from Bible study, and it was pretty late at night. The car in front of me made a U-turn from the right-hand lane crossing the left-hand lane, which I was

in. I was miraculously moved out of the path of a head on colli-
sion. It was the strangest thing. I hardly know how to explain
how it happened, except to say I was picked up and placed in
the right lane out of harm's way. There were no skid marks, no
loss of control. Everything happened in a split second, and yet
in slow motion. I can still picture it as though it were a recent
experience. Had I not been picked up and gently moved out
of the path of that vehicle, I would have gone over the edge of
the bridge, leaving my husband a widower and my children
without a mom. Thank you, God! Your arm is not shortened
on my behalf! ********

After that time, when the woman in the salon prayed
for me, I began to ponder my relationship with God and
His Son. Not as Father and Brother, but as Almighty,
All Powerful, and All Knowing. I questioned my understanding; I challenged His love. I challenged His ability
to protect me and what belonged to me. I questioned
my purpose in this world and His desire to give me
significance. Most of the time, I didn't believe He even
knew I was alive. How could He create significance for
me? Although I was living a life that indicated otherwise, there remained that still, small voice beckoning
me into the light.

My second experience with an overwhelming sense
of what Jesus did for me came when I was in the second trimester with my first born, Sarah. It was during
Easter time, when the Catholic church has ongoing

services recreating the death and resurrection of Jesus. During one of these services, heaven opened, and I realized I was a sinner. Not an ashamed and guilty sinner, but the kind of sinner who feels the compassion of another who can make a difference. For the first time in my Catholic upbringing, I felt like I was loved as a valuable part of the human race and known by God. I was significant! As that wooden cross with an image of Jesus was laid on the altar step, I began to cry. Everyone else blamed it on the pregnancy, but I knew better. The feeling lasted for a while, and then the cares of the world replaced my peace.

In 1982, I was taking serious inventory of my life. I graduated high school and was trained in a career that I was successful at. I married Bill. I encouraged Bill to get custody of his son Billy, birthed three children of my own, and began to seriously seek answers to the eternal question, "Why was I born?"

Most of my time, energy, and money was spent in finding the next experience that brought me recognition or the next shopping spree. Every purchase created for me a mask that looked like success. My children were disguised in name brands and latest trends. Looking at us from the outside, we looked like Norman Rockwell's picture of "Family."

The truth is, I wanted to invest time and energy in my marriage, but when I did, I was left longing. I needed my children to worship and fear me. They did the best they could, but nothing would have been enough to make me feel like I wasn't wasting my time. There was no amount of return that could do for me what I needed. I sacrificed much for the love of my children— I thought. They sacrificed a healthy home, which they eventually rebelled against. (Someday I may tell you about that, but not now.) It is enough to say, that the expectations on my family to meet my emotional needs was unrealistic. My love was self-centered and could never be satisfied.

*******A child's love can never replace the proper self-esteem of the parent. It cannot define a parent. It isn't supposed to. Relationships that are self-motivated leave no room for others to be who they are. There is no room to grow. The demands of the one in control dictate the gift and the giving, which can never be enough to satisfy spiritual hunger. It satisfies the lusts of the flesh and leaves you wanting more—not more stuff. It's never about stuff. Relationships are about the spirit. Self-centeredness leaves little or no room for God-centeredness. I was left hopelessly wanting and determined to find answers. ********************************

So, I did what I do best. I challenged a loving, trustworthy God to do for me what I couldn't do for myself. Of course, there was a catch. There's always a catch when you can't trust "men." After all, God is a father figure who is male. There was little respect or trust connected to these identities due to my experience of abuse and perversion from childhood.

If God failed to meet my expectations, which I imagined He would, I was going to leave my family and/or kill myself. I don't know if I would have carried out that threat, but a loving Father's first responsibility to His daughter is for safety. God lovingly protected me from myself. His word says that He is close to those with a broken heart and a contrite spirit. He is true to His word. What I didn't know then, but understand now, is that God's mercy beckons His children, and His grace meets them where they are. My ultimatum really had little to do with me and everything to do with God being Love. And yet, Love is all about me. Can you grasp it? I'm still trying!

That same week, I talked to my friend Yvonne. That wasn't unusual; it was something I did daily. However, this time, we talked about God— which was unusual. We often talked openly about our faith, but not about our needs connected to our faith. It seems she too had been seeking and, wouldn't you know, Bonnie, my co-worker from Snooty Fox who I decided knew everything about life and living, had an experience "just last night" that she shared with Yvonne. It seems she was dissatisfied with her life and went to see her lawyer to make up a will. She had decided to commit suicide based on her inability to justify her existence and satisfy her longing for a mate and for purpose. Fortunately, she didn't want her child to go without provision. Her lawyer talked to her about an "experience" he had that changed his life, and he encouraged Bonnie to attend a Bible study at the Shrine of Our Lady of The Snows. The Spirit of God met her there. Her feet had not yet touched the ground at the time she and Yvonne talked. God's timing is perfect! The attorney found purpose, which spoke to Bonnie's needs, and Bonnie's experience touched Yvonne's life, which touched my life.

The week after Bonnie attended the Bible Study at the Shrine, she offered to take us back with her. Her life had been changed so dramatically in one week's time that she wanted more. Yvonne and I agreed to meet her out there. I don't think I heard much of what was talked about during the study. I was distracted by my thoughts about the experience that was going to give me purpose and hope, which had not yet happened. So, after what seemed like an eternity, I found myself in a circle of people who were all putting their hands on me and praying.

One was saying, just let the words flow; another told me to wait on the Lord, another would encourage me to submit to the anointing as I felt the most incredible feeling of peace I have ever known. My tummy felt like an explosion and my throat swelled with something I couldn't swallow. I didn't know what was happening to me, but I liked it. People were all around speaking in languages I didn't know. I thought I was on fire from the inside out. Finally, I decided nobody was going to let me go home until something happened, and I opened my mouth and sounds of gibberish came forth. I began to cry and the people around me began to rejoice. I don't even know who they were. My knees were weak, and I felt like melting. Then, after much congratulations and pats on the back, we left. Just like that!

Yvonne and I drove together. Neither of us felt like going home just yet. The weight of the world was just lifted from our hearts; we felt free! We drove to the hamburger drive-in to talk through this experience neither of us understood or could explain in human terms. What we did know was that we no longer felt like smoking the cigarettes we lit, but we did it anyway. We laughed. We talked about peace and finding what we were looking for, wondering what we were supposed to do with it. AND...I felt there was something else.

I went to the doctor that same week. You guessed it! I was pregnant. Maggie was just three months old. This time, I was ready for a boy!

Bill's great-great-grandfather was named Isaac. I couldn't imagine a better name—laughter. For the first time in my life, I laughed from my heart, an innocent laugh born of the Spirit.

CHAPTER 6

Are You There, Lord?

Being born of the Spirit doesn't mean free from the body.

Although I revealed my experience with my husband, he was glad but doubtful that such a thing existed as speaking in tongues. That didn't discourage me from beginning to renew my mind or using and developing my language. I ravenously fed off the Word to nourish my spirit that had been neglected for so long. Transformation was a learning process. God is faithful! He that has begun a good work in you will complete it to the end. I didn't know how much time I had, but it didn't feel like enough. The days and nights were not long enough to undo the works of the enemy.

Although I got my work done and kept the kids clean and fed, I seemed to have more than enough time to devote to scripture reading. When I wasn't reading scripture, I was listening to Christian radio. I did not yet know good teaching from bad. Anything was better than nothing, and I let the Holy Spirit sort through it and teach me what I needed to know.

No one was safe from my enthusiasm. I loved the Lord and was so thankful to Him for giving me a purpose. However, not everyone shared my point of view. One of my sisters was critical, one was skeptical, and three turned deaf ears to my new-found faith. My mother was heartbroken. She couldn't understand why my Catholic upbringing wasn't enough, and there was no doubt in her mind that I was going to spend eternity in hell, because I suggested the Pope was a human being—perhaps no more full of the Holy Spirit than I. For the first time in twenty years, my mother lifted her hand to strike me. From that moment on, I never disrespected her beliefs again. It took a while, but I learned to appreciate all that I had been taught as the result of the education I received from Catholic school and my mother's example. God is faithful!

During those first years, I talked like a Christian talks, and I read scripture like Christians did. I even went to Bible study like Christians. Inside, like many Christians, I still felt the pains of loneliness as Bill and I maintained our separate positions about God and church-going. He was glad I had something that interested me. Asking him to participate was another story.

Doing what a lot of women do, I became a "secret agent of the Lord's army."

Being a secret agent requires one to do activities in secret. Secrecy between husband and wife is a tool of Satan to kill, steal, and destroy what God has put together. The one behind the walls fights against the one who belongs in the position of authority behind the wall barricade. Any breech in the "wall of protection" requires the agent to destroy the advances of the enemy by engaging in spiritual warfare. I stood on one side of salvation and my husband stood on the other. While I pretended to love, honor, and obey, behind his back I was rude, disrespectful, and ungrateful. I worshipped God for His many gifts and criticized Bill for not being a good provider—even though that wasn't true. I cried rivers of tears, because my husband was not surrendered to Jesus while demonizing his desires for intimacy. I could have avoided a lot of heartache if I had understood early on that Bill was not my enemy but my authority ordained by God to "tend and keep." Surrendering to Bill meant I had surrendered to God, since Bill was my covering. If I had known then that how I treat my husband is how I treat God, then I may have felt and acted differently. And just maybe, I may not have changed, since I had so many male issues to deal with. Trusting God, who I could not see, was an issue.

Bill, who I could see, was certainly not more trustworthy than God—according to me.

*******Man was created by the hand of God from the dust of the earth and God breathed life into his nostrils. The man was given the command to tend and keep what was entrusted to him, which was the garden and the woman. The woman was created to be a help by organizing and maintaining the contents within the parameters of what the man is tending and keeping. She is loved by her Maker, but not designed to communicate with God about authority and dominion. All information she receives comes through her covering, while walking in the cool of the evening with his Maker. The man and the woman are one (Eve didn't even get her name until after sin entered the garden.) The woman is taken from the side of man indicating that the man and the woman are one body—equal in all ways, but not above the head. She was created by a rib (that which protects his heart, emotions, and his lungs—breath of Life).

The woman, being a type of the flesh, is given the task of maintaining balance between the mind, will, and emotions, while creating strategy in the flesh. When the husband refuses to walk in the cool of the evening with his Maker, then the surrendered helpmate's position is to encourage him to reconnect with his authority and, thereby, regain control as the head of the man and woman. With a gentle and quiet spirit, she waits on God to confirm or redeem their circumstances and turn the heart of the man. This requires the woman to trust God, some-

thing I was not yet able to do. Of course, all of this is hindsight from years of studying Genesis 1,2 &3. **

What actually happened was, I continued to smoke. I screamed at my kids, and sometimes I cursed my husband. I drank on occasion—the wrong occasions with my girlfriends. And I dieted to find identity. My heart was bitter, and so were my words to those who I deemed as unsaved. I worked off and on in the salon (against my husband's wishes) to feel like I had some "independence" from this heathen I called husband. I could talk Bible with the best and gossip with the rest. My tongue was a rudder out of control, not yet tamed by the Spirit. I spent money we didn't have and ran up our credit cards to their limit. There is a bright side. "I" did manage to stop swearing. It was the least I could do. Besides, I didn't really want to swear anymore.

I wanted to do good, but I acted awful. It seemed I could not control much more than cussing. I loved God. I didn't trust Him, but I did love Him to the best of my ability. To my Christian friends, it must have looked quite the opposite. I am so grateful that God interpreted my heart and not my actions. I am so grateful that He gave me grace through my behavior while continually drawing me closer to Him.

Six years after I was born again, I decided it was time to make a decision. I had been straddling the fence since salvation, trying to decide where I would continue to worship. After 28 years, I decided I was no longer getting what I needed from the Catholic Church. I struggled with having an intercessor to reach God and, depending on whether I was good enough, maybe He wouldn't be too busy to send a saint on my behalf. There was a little church that seemed to spring up out of nowhere known as Shiloh Rock. I didn't understand why it was called Shiloh Rock when it was located in Belleville, but I didn't hold that against them. (That was only funny if you knew that the town of Shiloh is located next to Belleville and the church was located in Belleville). I was so ignorant about scripture. But, God...

*******I removed my children from parochial school (a decision I regret today) and set out to gain what I felt was withheld from me in Catholicism: relationship. Today, I don't believe God esteems one religion over another and relationship depends on the individual. I don't believe religion is God's best for His children. I do believe that God meets us where we are. He does His best work in those who are surrendered to His Spirit, regardless of where we are when we surrender. We don't have to disrespect our roots, nor do we have to reject our background of faith. Today, I am grateful for what I learned foundationally in the Catholic Church. In hindsight, I believe I neglected my children's foundational understanding of God by rejecting my upbringing in the Catholic church. Today, I understand that no matter where one begins, the ending can be satisfying in Jesus without getting stuck. My advice to you *is to go fellowship and make connections where you are that serve your family.* *******

This small group of believers welcomed me with open arms, and I grew in grace. While I believe that couples would be better off if they attended church together, it doesn't always work out that way. It wasn't God's best for me and the children to attend church without our covering, but I did what I knew to do and stumbled and fumbled my way into redemption by the grace of God. If I had listened to my husband, I don't know what would have happened. I believe that God is a redeeming God, and I have many memories to prove it. Even though I misunderstood Bill's authority and non-attendance in church as apathy; I decided I could do what I wanted, and God would be happy for me.

It had been five years since my experience with the Spirit of God attending Shiloh Rock Church. I felt like I had taken one step toward redemption while the rest of me remained bound by the shame and guilt of my past, and now my present, which continually created consequences for the unhealthy choices I made. I was becoming disenchanted with the Spirit, who promised so much more. Not that I hadn't grown, because I had. Peace often prevailed. However, the time had come when I needed to surrender more. I didn't know why, but I felt like I was walking inside a hamster wheel watching the world pass me by as I continued to work hard at becoming a new creation.

Once again, and true to my nature, I hung my fleece in the form of a challenge. "God, I need you to be real. I am so tired of living on the edge of a miracle trying to make You into something I need to satisfy me and give me purpose. I'm tired of not having fun doing it. Prove yourself to be who You say You are, and I will lay down my cigarettes to seek You!" That was about 10:00 in the evening.

Jim Spillman was speaking at a local restaurant the next day, and one of the church members called and asked me to join them. I had heard him speak before and knew that he operated in the Holy Spirit, so I was enthusiastic. I fasted and prayed the whole day having high expectations that God would not let me down. Some doubt continued in the back of my mind. After all, God is male, and I am not all that valuable, I told myself. Then I would pray with my prayer language to stop the negative thoughts. By the way, I never had a desire for another cigarette. From the moment I made that commitment until today—twenty-five years later. I was as free from the effects of nicotine as I was the night I became born again and Spirit filled five years earlier. God instantly delivered me, and I didn't realize it until the next few days when it hadn't crossed my mind to light up. Isn't God gracious!

Well, we went to the meeting. Spillman was dynamic, as usual. He began and ended without so much as a nod in my direction. With a broken heart, I got up and began to walk out knowing that this was going to be the last time I encountered God. The other part of that fleece/challenge was that if God could not prove Himself, I was going to jump into sin with both feet. I intended to leave my kids, divorce my husband, or live in the pursuit of whatever made me happy and with whomever I wanted. Perhaps, I thought, there was no point in living. Although I didn't want to do any of that, I worked really hard to be someone different without what I thought should look like success. I still hated me, and I was sure God must feel the same way sometimes. What I wanted, and what most people in serious emotional pain want, is to be free from the pain of their past. Like a ball and chain, my past shackled me to the shame and the guilt that continued to haunt me.

The way I saw it, there wasn't much more I could do to destroy myself and my family. I shopped daily, I cleaned none stop. I went to my mom's house to escape my own. My sister was living with Mom at the time, so I involved myself with anything that took my mind off some of my circumstances. I was growing weary of that also. Perhaps the solution was to escape...whatever that meant. God, I was tired!

All of these thoughts penetrated my peace as I approached the door to leave the meeting. Someone called my name. One of the guys I had come with was talking to a friend of his that pastored a church in St. Charles. As I was being introduced to him, I reached out to shake his hand. He extended his other hand, which I took, as he looked me in the eyes and asked, "What are you so angry about?" It felt like his hands had attached themselves to mine, burning into my flesh. If I could have, I would have escaped right then and there, but I couldn't seem to free myself from this guy's grip. How dare this **man** ask me why I was angry? Then, he began to say words that were comforting and caring. Words I didn't understand with my ears but spoke volumes to my heart. Finally, he released my hands, and I don't think my feet touched the ground for the next year.

God cares!!! He cares about me and my stupid challenges. What a relief! God heard me! He loves me!

That night, I also found out that the church I had been attending was slowly falling apart. There were some secrets and some inappropriate handling of the money. All that didn't matter now. There was no doubt where I was going. I had a church to go to from now on!

There were many victories and many mistakes I experienced as I began attending the church in St. Charles. The next year was a whirlwind of teaching, and absorbing, and studying, and ministry, and idols, and wrong teaching, and demons, and deliverance, and marriage problems, and money problems, fasting, and praying, kid problems, and good memories created with kids and husband ...It was the best year of my life, thus far—and the worst. Much to the chagrin of my husband, I began attending the church in St. Charles.

*******The closer you move toward God, the closer God gets. That's His promise and He is a keeper of His promises regardless of the mistakes along the way. I made many!*******

That was over twenty years ago. I was a different person then. Desperate for the things of God, I was easily influenced. I wanted to be noticed and significant. So much so, that I mistakenly befriended the pastor and interpreted it as being increasingly significant to God. This man taught the Word, after all. Surely, he had the ear of God in a greater way than I. Being close to him would allow me to be noticed by God. That understanding carried over from the Catholic church, which influenced me to believe there was a special connection between priests and God that I would never experience as a lay person. Here was my chance.

I did everything I was told. The pastor was really big into nutrition and fitness. I learned everything I could about eating right and working out. I had just quit smoking, and contrary to popular beliefs, I lost close to fifty pounds. I worked out daily, walked anywhere from five to ten miles a day. I drank supplements made of barley and took vitamins that were all natural, which promised to process fully in your system offering the most benefit for the money. I ate only fruit for breakfast and never mixed proteins with carbs or fat with fruit. Not once did processed sugar cross my lips or bleached white bread or rice either. Everything I ate was natural and unprocessed, despite the opposition I received from my family. Faithfully, I served at the altar of my new addiction in an effort to be somebody and to please the pastor and supplement his income with the nutritional products I used.

I attended church on Sunday morning and Sunday night. I went on Wednesday night and often on Saturday morning for Bible study and ministry preparation. Bill wouldn't have minded so much, but each trip put eighty miles on the vehicle we were driving at the time. In order to get to Church on time Sunday morning, we would leave the house no later than 6:30 a.m. The children and I didn't return home until about 8:00 p.m. Rain, snow, hail, or dark of night couldn't keep me from my destiny. I was racking up the god points!

When Bill would complain about the time I was spending away from home, I told him he didn't understand. When he realized the amount of weight I had lost and that my confidence was rising, he questioned my integrity. My response was to reassure him that no man could lure me away from his side. Meanwhile, I was glad to be free from this unsaved man who continually desired me and showered me with compliments in between the criticisms about my new faith. When his jealousy would get the best of him, and he would refuse to let me use the car, I borrowed one or got a ride from one of the couples from Shiloh Rock who also decided to attend. Once

Again, I was attending a church where the congregation was small. In my mind, it kept the competition down which suited me fine.

Pastor was invested in deliverance, which was a big movement at the time. The whole church made plans to go to Arkansas to the camp that boasted great revival due to their success in casting out demons. When we went to the Deliverance Camp in Arkansas, I took the kids with me. Bill wasn't interested. I scrimped and saved to afford that experience that I was sure was the answer to my heart's cry to be free from the shame and guilt of my past. We drove as a caravan, so when my money was "stolen" after the first one hundred miles on the road, the other drivers all pitched in and saved the day. I was still pretty naïve and entrusted my money to the pastor. What was I thinking? The pastor insisted that one of the men, who was not well known by the group had taken it, but I wonder...

Anyway, the deliverance camp was as you might suspect. Pointing fingers at little girls with pierced ears and speaking ugly "prophecy" about their evil destiny because of their ears being pierced. Pictures of owls and heart shapes had the potential to lure unwanted activity into my home due to the open door that these shapes and figures allowed. Having a cabbage patch doll was evil due to the representation of the adoption process. By allowing my girls to play with these, I was allowing them to play with the demons that inhabited them. Almost anything and everything that Bill and I had purchased for our children over the years must be gotten rid of due to what it allows and/or represents. I couldn't give it away because I would be subjecting others to what I was ridding myself and my family of. Nothing was safe! Satan and his imps lurked in the shadow of opportunity. In every toy and material possession that bore the mark of the world, Satan attached himself to snatch God's best from the safety of the Spirit. Boy, was I naive!

Yes, Bill questioned me. Yes, the kids cried and screamed and told me they didn't understand. Yes, the opposition was great, and the accusations, criticisms, and judgments were unending. How could I have been so gullible to believe as those who preached this stuff? Did they really believe that Satan is more powerful than God? How did I not understand that if I was embarrassed to speak out loud the position I had taken about the things I had destroyed in the name of deliverance, that the practice was questionable? How did I not know that my loyalty should have been greater to my family and their well-being than to those who tragically influenced my walk with God. Because my husband wasn't born again, I thought I couldn't trust him to speak the wisdom of God. What I didn't understand, was that God's command to my husband had never been rescinded. What I didn't understand, was that whatever mistakes Bill made in following the command, God could be trusted to redeem. I didn't listen to that still, small voice inside me, I listened to the so-called authorities which cost us a lot of heart ache and money by throwing away toys, clothes, linens, pictures, and jewelry.

Then, one day, I decided I had had enough. Just like that, I had enough of Bill, I had enough of financial problems. I had enough of criticism and judgments that came from being different. Certainly, God did not intend for me to live in such torment. Little did I know that the torment was self-inflicted as well as other-inflicted. However, I made up my mind to leave Bill and, along with that decision, I made the worst mistake of my life—to walk out and leave my kids at home. Financially they would be better off, I told myself. They could stay in school and not have to leave their comfy beds. They wouldn't have to leave their friends. Besides, I wasn't going anywhere they could go. I wasn't going to my mom's but to one of the church member's apartment forty-five miles away.

When I arrived, I was welcomed with some apprehension as no one was willing to take on potential problems that come with separation, especially not the man that so often took me into the presence of God—my pastor. Instead, he treated me as though I was wrong, and Bill was worth whatever it took to maintain our marriage. What??? What happened to the encouragement to be the best for God? Did I miss something? I thought that to be unequally yoked allowed for me to separate, especially since Bill was so difficult to live with.

This man that molded and shaped me for ministry was now telling me I was not hearing God? *Now,* I was angry! Christians aren't supposed to turn their backs on other Christians and encourage them to return to *'Egypt'*—the place of bondage. *Especially* Christians who stood in the place of God!

Foolishly, I believed the *man* was *God,* and I allowed his control to manifest and come between me and my husband. Foolishly, I believed my decisions were being orchestrated by God and refused to believe that leaving my husband was a mistake. Foolishly, I misinterpreted the fear of responsibility as concern. Desperately, I wanted to believe that I was safe with this man-god and that my best interest was at the center of his motive. What an awakening! It was painful, but God, who is rich in mercy, gave me insight and understanding into His plans that become perverted in the hands of man. When loyalty and gratitude turn into idolatry and debt-collecting, it is easy to fall prey to control. More than once, I fell into the trap of control because I worshipped the creation instead of the Creator.

Downcast and broken-hearted, I got in the car that would take me back to my family. It was a long and quiet ride full of tension. I was confused and angry. The pastor was scared. (I'm not giving him the benefit of the doubt here. He may have been truly concerned about my circumstances. Even if he wasn't, God intervened on my behalf and I went back where redemption could prevail.) Bill met us at the door with open arms and criticism. Pastor spoke to him about my intentions, my pain, and my position. Bill listened and agreed that to reconcile was the best solution to this dilemma. Pastor left with a promise to meet with us on a weekly basis until we felt like we could take care of ourselves. That lasted about two weeks. The pain was greater than us and the responsibility for our pain became a burden for the pastor. I told you I was naïve.

It wasn't long before my time at that church was coming to an end. The members were needing more options and pastor was needing more stability, which can be interpreted as more money. It took me a little while to get over that experience. Not blaming God for drawing me in and "dumping me" was my greatest hurdle. Learning to figure out where God begins and man continues is a tedious and torturous process that can make or break the spirit of a person. It can also keep that person stuck emotionally and spiritually. Thank You, God for being consistently who You say You are!

CHAPTER 7

Why Me and When?

A year after my experiences across the river, I began attending a church pastored by a member of the previous church I attended. He was also the man that introduced me to the pastor in St. Charles. In my brokenness, I returned to a place that allowed me my pain. Whether by the Spirit or speculation, they understood I was fragile. If they judged, they were not vocal about it. Their behavior didn't indicate it either. They didn't say a lot to me, but they included me and gave me space to heal and seek God in my own way. Maybe God created that little band of saints on my behalf. Regardless of why things happened the way they did, or why that church seemed to last only until I was able to "stand" again, I don't know. What I do know is that God orchestrates people for the benefit of people to prove that He is Love. That's what I needed, and that's what I got: God and the healing resources of His love. There is something to be learned from every situation. It's better for me to let God reveal it so I can move on. Otherwise, I know me; I'll get stuck by analyzing it to death. God being who He is, I am sure the others received what they asked for as well.

I don't remember a whole lot about that time except that I was self-absorbed because of unresolved pain that compounded the initial pain of shame and guilt I carried from my childhood. Regardless of the pain, I functioned as a mother and wife to the best of my ability. The radio and tapes were my closest friends.

Every opportunity I had to share my story I did. There were a lot of opportunities since I spent so much time doing Bible studies, and Bible conferences, and Church. I shared so much of my pain with so many people without good results, that becoming reclusive seemed the best solution. I decided that it was time to snap out of "it" and start doing what it was I needed to do as unto the Lord for the best results. My favorite scripture was from Psalms 26:3: "Lean not on your own understanding, but in all your ways acknowledge Him and He will direct your path." Putting me on hold and investing in my kids gave me the motivation to invest in life again.

Besides, I was tired. I was tired of regurgitating my painful past and not receiving the answers I needed to settle my stomach. As soon as I told my tale, people would look at me as though I disgusted them for making a mess on their carpet. They didn't know any more what to do with me then I did. So, I would scoop up my 'regurgitated mess' and go home saying, "Next time I would get some answers."

Shame and guilt require answers that sort out the experiences of the hemorrhaged soul. I bombarded heaven with my questions. It was not easy to receive answers on the run. Just in case God wasn't paying attention or my suspicions were correct, and He was disgusted by me, I was in a constant state of turmoil that required all my time and attention to concentrate. My mind raced between one thought and another, between the past failures and the future intentions. Just in case I was right about me being unworthy of God's resources, I ran. I ran from my present state of mind and circumstances where the presence of the Father and Son reside. It was just too painful to ponder.

Often, I have described myself as a four-drawer file cabinet that was under-utilized and over-stuffed. It only took sixteen years of walking with God (actually the Holy Spirit) and many encounters with his people to sort through it all. As I "walked" I learned. As I learned, I was able to refile old messages and experiences until the file cabinet was cleared of its clutter. Each file was neatly placed in its proper place, the file marked, "Blood of Jesus," "Cancelled," "Forgiveness," "Grace," and "Mercy." I leaned not on my understanding and kept moving toward God, even though I was confused about who I was to Him and who He was to me.

In the back of my mind, I was convinced that my debt was not cancelled because I continued to reap the consequences of the shame and guilt of past, now present, and probably future choices. In my mind, there was no hope for my redemption while, in my heart, the voice of the Holy Spirit spoke about peace and restoration. My spirit was so far out of alignment, and the layers of my soul and body had become so calloused, that the words of the Comforter took a while to penetrate. Then the process of what I heard had to be proven to who, in my mind, I had become to survive. The conversations about who I thought I was, compared to who God said I was, conflicted with reality. God is faithful and the work He began continued.

Thankfully, by the grace of God, Joyce Meyer had begun a ministry on the Illinois side of the river. Every Tuesday I rushed to receive whatever nourishment I could from this woman with the deep voice. There wasn't a time in those meetings that she didn't seem to speak directly to me. Many of her past circumstances paralleled my own—sexual abuse, isolation, inability to trust men, shame, guilt, identity crisis...Some of her favorite sayings mirrored my heart, as I often asked God the same questions, "why and when?"

Why was I abused? When will I be free from the effects of it?

A lot of teaching during those early years of my salvation **revolved** around pain and suffering "allowed" by God.

Allowed is in quotes because, today, I understand that God is never the source of my pain. God will never overstep the boundaries of free will—mine or someone else's against mine. Today, I understand that pain and suffering cannot always be explained, except to say that it is the result of living in a fallen world. Most of all, I learned that guilt played a major role in my shameful experiences when I developed behaviors and defenses to survive the shame and protect myself.

Early on, I *believed* that God allowed trauma, and crisis, and bad things so that later I could create ministry around helping others survive the pain of abuse. As far as I was concerned, I qualified for that position.

Emotional pain and suffering were my best friends. The choices I made, because of that suffering, caused me much physical pain in the form of spending, relationships with males and females, being overweight, starving myself to lose weight, tumors, diverticulosis... If anyone qualified for bringing God some glory for what they survived, it was me. I believed there was no other explanation for any of the bad things that happened except to glorify God, who would do exceedingly and abundantly above all I could ask, or think, or imagine as long, as I didn't lean on my own understanding, but acknowledged Him to direct my path. (Still the victim. Not being free from guilt and shame but ignoring the roots of shame and focusing on the fruit of it. All the while proclaiming that everything happens for a reason. Well, that may be true, but it is not true that everything that happens is God's will.)

Here is how I reasoned. As I am writing, it's hard for me to follow. I hope you understand it better than I and are delivered from it if it too is your story.

I was not just a victim of incest and my own behavior to survive the abuse, I had become a victim of God. I didn't trust myself to make choices, and I didn't believe that God trusted me either. Because He didn't trust me, He must be creating **all** the circumstances in my life. All the time I sabotaged God's best efforts for restoration by "doing it myself" and blaming God for the results. I struggled to give up control, and yet fought myself to surrender. I reasoned that I was protecting myself from the enemy while rejecting reason. After all, wasn't it God who created me to be used, abused, and rejected? Why would He ask me *not* to lean on my own understanding otherwise? Wasn't it He that created my value when I was born? By the way, I rejected that teaching that said if I was the only person alive, Jesus would have died on my behalf.

No, I told myself, He made me for His glory. Not making me a valuable vessel of honor was part of His plan. I just had to be the best dishonorable vessel He ever made. If I were to be the best vessel I was created to be, then I couldn't be faulted for making a mess.

On the other hand, if I didn't complete the circle of problem-pain-direct my path-survive-teach others to survive-give God glory, then I would be at fault. When I could lift *myself* above the circumstances of how I was created, then I could give Him the praise for His ability to strengthen me so I could continue doing His work. It isn't difficult to twist the scriptures to make 'sense' of life. Oftentimes, it was my only way of making sense of my reality.

CHAPTER 8

Answers

I had so much information and so little ability to sort through it to come up with an answer that would alleviate my pain. Was I to carry it until eternity? Well then, hurry up Jesus! What I heard from the pulpit, what I read, and what I experienced was always in conflict. It didn't appear that others had any better understanding than I did. Why else would I interpret what I heard not as a solution, but another "doctrine" of faith.

There were scriptures I read that confirmed my belief. God is all-powerful, all-knowing, and everywhere all the time. How could a loving God allow such torment to inhabit His creation? How could He allow an innocent child to suffer the hemorrhaging of the soul, as I did, without intervening? He was Sovereign—there was no doubt about that. God sent a Savior—no doubt about that. Savior I understood. Unfortunately, Father, brother, friend, I did not understand. The thing I especially struggled to understand was Love.

According to some experts, my understanding about God comes from my relationship with my earthly parents. If my understanding comes from my relationship with my biological dad, then accepting God as Father would have to come later, when I could figure out my confusion. (I believe my dad did the best he could, but he fell way short of keeping me safe, making me feel significant, and offering me unconditional love.)

Putting my life in the hands of a "male" God I could not trust, and calling Him Abba, wasn't at all appealing. Putting my life in the hands of Jesus and calling Him brother was another questionable practice. He could be my Savior. I knew I couldn't do that on my own—I tried. (I almost killed myself trying to work for my salvation). Although my brother functioned biologically as a man, he was just a teenager. He died before he was 21. Regardless of his ability, or his chronological age, my brother was a scary figure I had not yet reconciled. He was the product of my dad, who never told me or showed me he loved me. Both my dad and my brother always made me feel like I needed a chaperone to be in their presence, just in case there was an intent to cross moral boundaries. Have you ever been in the presence of someone that made you feel like you wanted to shower after talking to them? That was my dad and brother.

That's why the third party of the Godhead was so significant for me. That's why I readily received the surrendering of myself to the Spirit with evidence of speaking in tongues. I knew nothing about the baptism of the Holy Spirit, but that experience proved that He heard me, and I was His. I had proof at that moment that God knew I existed and that I had a purpose. I knew that whatever answers I needed had to be given supernaturally. Desperate to have a healthy, happy, safe, relationship with God, I hoped He was the God I heard about, and not the God of my understanding.

I knew about God. I knew about Jesus. As a matter of fact, my Catholic upbringing gave me an excellent foundation about that understanding. There just had to be more. I decided I was done trying to figure it out and just accepted what I was given. God knew what I needed and offered His Holy Spirit to "tend and keep" me in my spiritual walk over the next seventeen years, until He could reveal to me what I wanted to know. The revelation would take place line upon line, an exchange of my facts for His truth .

Here's some side notes about forgiveness that would be appropriate here. I heard and practiced forgiveness toward my dad, my mom, and my brother, even though my brother was dead at the time. Jack Hayford says, "If you want forgiveness, be general, but if you want freedom, be specific."

I forgave, generally, because I told myself that I didn't want to dredge up the past. It all happened in the past—let it stay there. Besides, those I needed to forgive had already died.

*******The problem with blanket forgiveness is that the ugly details are ignored. Those details (facts) expose the individual's truth about their experiences. When the truth is revealed, then responsibility for transgressions are realized, and the behaviors one develops to survive them are recognized. Recognizing the truth of the individual, and exchanging it for God's truth, is what sets the individual free. Adam and Eve knew they had to cover their nakedness and chose to do it with garments they created from fig leaves. God exchanged their temporary covering for His eternal one, shedding blood to accomplish it. *******

Because I was unable, or not ready, to take responsibility for the part I played in the abuse, I remained paralyzed by the guilt and shame which kept me in bondage. Remember that scripture that says God will not give you more than you are able to bear without making a way of escape? That applies here. The last 17 years as a Christian were lived under the shadow of His wings when the Holy Spirit was allowing me to know only what I could handle. Every revelation was filtered through the love and comfort of the Holy Spirit. He protected me from the devastating effects of finding out too much too soon. I was fragile, and God understood. The Holy Spirit protected from what could potentially "destroy" me if revealed too quickly.

The forgiveness I gave was a blanket forgiveness, and my expectations were for specific freedom although I didn't feel it. I've learned a few things since then. While I asked "Why" and "When," I continued to hold onto the teachings and conclusions drawn by those who "knew" more than I. What they said sounded good at the time. I heard it, and it allowed me to continue my pursuit of freedom, but it didn't do much for my trust level.

What I concluded about what God "allows" caused me to question His intent. If God was using trauma and painful experiences to bring Him glory, what would He use next to satisfy that purpose? The idea of not knowing created more anxiety about whether God was trustworthy or not. As I wrestled with God, I continued to listen to Christian radio, read the Bible, and read books about evangelists who had struggled and overcome their experiences and trials.

Tapes—now, there's a good resource. I didn't go anywhere that I didn't have my tapes playing. Psalms on tape gave me a hopeful edge. I could read at home and listen in the car. I became a student of the Psalms when I figured out David's weaknesses didn't keep him from being a "man after God's own heart"—a declaration made by God Himself. I had to find out what David did, and what he had that I needed, so that I, too, could get God's attention. I felt a little hopeful, wondering if I was good enough or bad enough to be noticed by my "Father."

CHAPTER 9

Maybe Now

Much time had gone by, almost nine years. My life was not without circumstance (but now is not the time to talk about a lot of it as it involves child rearing). I'll leave that for another book in order to stay focused on the exchange.

The little church I attended stopped meeting at a rented facility and began meeting at the home of the pastor, which was his mother and father's home. Our little congregation was content for the time being but, after about a year, one by one we began to find other places to worship.

It was time to start thinking about my children, who needed some God attention. They were getting some Bible stories, but nothing consistent. No matter how small a congregation, adding four children to any number would be a reason to create a program. Unfortunately, there has to be a teacher willing to devote time and energy to the program. There was one other family that attended who had two kids. When they didn't show up, there was no Sunday school. I was doing the best I could at home teaching them scripture and stories about God, but I fell short.

Everything I seemed to do fell short of God's best, the way I saw it. So, I used material things to fill the black hole of need while I tried to live a life that would make God proud of me. The two are not compatible or comparable. Unsanctified flesh is an enemy of God, and there is nothing that can change that. Trust me when I say, I did everything I could to make it happen. Something I recently figured out, was that although the unsanctified flesh is an enemy to God, God still loves the whole me and uses and teaches through surrendered flesh for the benefit of others. Rethink rejecting your flesh because God hates it. God created all of you and loves all of you. Reaping the blessings of that love is ongoing and becomes greater as the flesh becomes aligned under the soul with the spirit in authority.

During that nine-year period of time, we moved. After twelve years of renting, the pressure from family and friends to own a house was more than we could escape. Besides, the landlady sold the house we were renting to her newly married daughter. We had one month to pack up and leave.

The house we bought was a really good deal, almost $20,000 below the appraisal price. Bill was doing well at work and the Army Reserves. The children were content.

We lived in that home for two years before it began to rain—not the Holy Spirit kind of rain, but gray skies, lightning and thunder rain. After two months of off and on rain, the carpet in the downstairs bathroom was wet. Easy enough to fix, we pulled up the carpet and replaced it with tile. Year two brought a little more drama and clean up. By the fifth year, and the fifth clean-up with a remodel, we were suing the city and walking away from our first home that fell into foreclosure. Seven years after we bought that home, we were moving out.

It started downstairs. Someone flushed the toilet, then the drain began to gurgle. I think the first time it was just rainwater. Year after year, it became increasingly clear that rainwater was not the only water bubbling up in our basement through the shower, the drain, and the toilet. The fifth and final year of our experience, it seemed like the neighborhood sewer was rerouted into our basement. By the time it stopped, there was almost two feet of pollution contaminating all the newly remodeled rooms where the girls slept, where the family gathered, and where the laundry was done.

The first time, the rug was soaked and smelly. Easy enough. We settled for cement floors and throw rugs. The next time, we used a little bleach to stop the water from creating mold in the drywall recently installed and replaced some bedding and curtains. Each season required more work and replacement than the last. By the time we realized we were not going to get any help from the city, the basement flooded five times. Five times we cleaned up and remodeled.

The problem was determined to have been caused by a faulty and/or broken sewer system that was unable to accommodate the amount of rain during this time of year. The problem originated from the drain in the street—the city's property. Our house sat in the lowest part of the subdivision. As the rain came, it accumulated in the manhole. The overflow created a problem for the city sewers which, in turn, created a problem for the homeowners. Water flows downhill, along with a lot of other things—right into our basement!

Our sewer lines were intact but, in order to stop the back flow, a valve needed to be installed. That would have fixed some of the problem, but not all. The city's excuse was "If they fixed our problem the whole neighborhood would expect help." What??? How could they refuse to take responsibility? This wasn't a problem we had created. It was the problem of inept city engineers not creating a sewer system to accommodate the subdivision.

We were so frustrated, and sad, and broken, and angry and...Where was the city when we bought this home to tell us the potential damage and frustration that awaited us. Why didn't someone tell us that living in the lowest part of the subdivision was hazardous to our health and finances? And by the way, where was God? Evidently, there was a lesson we needed to learn, and God was using this experience to bring us to awareness. That's what I heard, and that's what I believed. Everything happens for a reason!

Maybe I was paying for the years of unforgiveness toward my mom, dad, and brother. Maybe it was greed, weakness, rage...Or perhaps, seeking God across the river, and the problems, and pain connected to that drama was the problem. I should be glad my first born was not taken. Just maybe, what I always believed was true—God had created me to be used, abused, and discarded. Bill and I were in turmoil within our spirit, soul, and bodies. There seemed to be lots of questions and too few answers.

The fifth year, the rain came and the damage was worse than all the previous years. At first, we closed the basement door. It stayed that way for a week. Eventually, I knew we would have to brave the smell and the floating feces, but not yet. I wasn't ready. I didn't know if I would ever be ready again. Bill was surely not ready. He was dealing with his own painful circumstances.

I had become a cleaning and remodeling genius after five years of experience. There was nothing left to do but open the door and brave this new opportunity to "give God the glory." We opened the door and walked down the first few steps for the first time since the flood. What we saw devastated us, and we sat down and cried. The water had risen to the third step, along with everything you can imagine that comes from a sewer. *I couldn't do it anymore.* Bill's frustration and stress peaked due to a culmination of experiences since moving.

We called the city, the Environmental Protection Agency, our mortgage holders, and FEMA. Each agreed that our situation was hazardous. Each agreed that we should get some legal help. FEMA even offered us some money to quick fix the problem, but then what? We contacted our attorney who said we had a good case, but due to the circumstances that had broken my husband's spirit, we would recover nothing from the lawsuit. In fact, after all was said and done, we decided the solution to this final straw was to file bankruptcy— once again.

Let me explain bankruptcy.

We filed bankruptcy two times in a five-year period. Bill and I were living beyond our means, Bill was transitioning into a new job with the Army. The job fell through. The second time we filed was due to loss of job and loss of hope because of the flooding in the basement.

Filing under any chapter of bankruptcy creates a catch 22 situation that offers little by way of recovering losses received from any legal action. As long as your file is open, it is impossible to collect from any financial institution for any reason until all debts are paid. Even though the city decided to settle out of court in our favor, the debt created by uncontrolled living, loss of job, and sewer damage created a black hole. The money we "won" went to our creditors. When you file bankruptcy twice, there is little you can do but surrender all debt and assets. Before it was over, I ended up in the hospital, which I shall explain later. For now, I will tell you that at the end of a seven-year battle, we left our first home financially broke and spiritually broken to live in my sister's basement.

Here is the story of Bill's pain during those first few years. While we were still living in our first bought home, there was a glimmer of hope. A slot for active duty opened up for Bill in the United States Army Reserve Command. He was ready. Bill would work as a full-time Lt. Colonel. Maybe now he could put the past behind him and find a new identity of respect.

Soon after the opening of a position, war broke out in the Middle East and Desert Storm began under the first President Bush. Although that may not sound hopeful to some, to a military man who has trained his whole life to uphold and defend this country and the constitution it was founded on... well, it was a dream come true. He was well respected in the military and built a reputation of integrity and character while accumulating rank.

As a young man, very early in his career, Bill was hired by the phone company. Bill's dad encouraged him to stay with the phone company and do weekend drills with the Army Reserves, thereby having the best of both worlds. Wanting to please his father, he kept his civilian job. Finally, after twenty-five years, he could retire from the phone company and live his dream of becoming active military. He could rid himself of the regrets held by being practical. We could rid ourselves of surmounting debt and incredible loss to regain some dignity. We put all our hope in this opportunity.

Then, Bill's unit was designated to go to the Middle East. Not only did he see this as a fulfillment of his dreams, he viewed it as a means to an end of the pervasive darkness that threatened to overtake him as I became less comforting and the children began to suffer from the consequences of all our bad choices. Honestly, I was a little scared and, at the same time, mad. Although I didn't care if he stayed or went off to the desert in the Middle East, I was angry that I was going to have to stay and clean up our mess. Can you imagine thinking that way?

Remember the tick story? I was hurting and felt there was nowhere to turn. I needed something from my husband he couldn't give me. He needed something from me, and I didn't want to give it. Really, I wasn't any more able than he was to give what I didn't possess—love.

In the meantime, I spoke truth about trusting God and silently battled the double minded demons that tried to convince me there was no God. Determined to prove those demons wrong, I continued to seek Him. Actually, there wasn't much I cared about except my kids and seeking God, even though I struggled to make sense of how He operated.

Then more bad news. Deployment was put on hold. Bill's unit was taken off the list for unknown reasons. As long as Bill remained in the Reserves, there was hope that he would be deployed and become active. I would be free to have control. Finally, he could do what it is he had trained his whole military career to do. I could do what I wanted. Sounds good, but that's not the way it happened. Thank God!

A second time, we got word that my husband's unit was called into action then, once again, withdrawn from the list of those to be deployed. Okay... I was glad. He wasn't, but secretly I was—not because he didn't have to put himself in harm's way for the preservation of our family and freedom, but because I thought if I couldn't escape our dilemma, then neither could he. Served him right!

Our emotions, my emotions, were all over the place. Next year was an election year. The political scene was about to change. President Clinton was elected. Along with cutting the military budget, the Missouri Democratic party made some changes also. Politics play a large role in the military. Unfortunately, the lives of the those that serve get lost in the shuffle. The slot previously held by Army Reserve was designated for the National Guard and Bill got bumped. Then, the president cut the military budget. Bill worked a couple of months in the position he was promised and then we were right back where we started. Knowing that Bill was without civilian employment, his best friend continued to acquire short stints on our behalf. We could still be spared the consequences of too much spending, compounded by too many bad experiences, and come out unscathed. There was no hope of fulfillment for a career in the military under these circumstances. Anger turned into depression. After 30 years with the United States Army Reserves, Bill retired. We still had Bill's phone company retirement to live on while he searched for another position. Unfortunately, his retirement was received in one lump sum and ended up being less than his total earnings for a year. It didn't last long.

Two times Bill received an alert to ready his command. Two times he received word that his command was put on hold—indefinitely. He was out of a job and out of steam—again. This time the military (the cash cow, the golden idol) had let him down. Too many obstacles to overcome in too short a time. Despair replaced hope. My heart was softened toward him because of what I knew the military meant to him. To the best of my ability, I tried to comfort him. Then, we decided it was time to do something else.

We went to the State to receive some help for groceries and possibly for rent. Did you know that you can't get grocery money, and/or rent money, or utility money if you own a vehicle worth more than $2,000? You don't even have to own it. If you are paying for it, and it's in your possession, the government wants you to sell it. Since we just purchased the minivan shortly before all the crisis, it would have been a lose/lose situation to sell it. The moment it was driven off the car lot, it diminished in value more than we owed. Besides, how was I supposed to transport five children, me, and Bill without a large vehicle to accommodate us all? Nothing was making sense, and I refused to leave until we got some help.

All I knew was I had five kids to feed and no way of doing it. Where were we to live? I guess the case workers have heard it all and decided it wasn't their problem. The best they could do for us at the time was an emergency disbursement for food. Thank God!

We got the names of the local food pantries, which required the last pay stub of previous employment. We were subjected to a lecture about some who "try to take advantage of the system." We were questioned about the length of time in between employment and seeking employment, as well as options for work. Although I was able to "shop," I was cautioned.

Talk about feeling like a nobody failure! I was hurting so bad I didn't have it in me to feel empathy for my husband. As for God, I thought He was on vacation and forgot to take me. At the very least, He could have notified me. When Jesus said, "My God, my God, why have you forsaken me?" I felt that I knew what he was feeling. We thought it was the lowest point of our lives.

During this six-year period of time, we bought a new home, Bill lost his job, we filed bankruptcy, we had two minivans, one of which was repossessed, and our house was in foreclosure. We won a lawsuit to recover our losses but collected nothing from it. We left our first home, which ended up in foreclosure, and we lived in my sister's basement. Our family was split, because we couldn't provide a place for them to stay. It seemed like we couldn't get a break—or food stamps.

At the end of the seven-year period, before we moved, I began working for Tony. I was barely making enough to buy groceries. My son, Isaac, had a friend who lived behind us. His friend's dad just took over a local salon and knew I did hair. My license lapsed, so there was little else I could do except make appointments and clean the restrooms. I didn't care. Tony was a good man but didn't understand the idiosyncrasies of stylists. *(Just a little advice; If you aren't familiar with the hair business and the mood swings of creative people then don't buy a salon. Having the loyalty of the stylist is far more lucrative than trying to control them into submission. At three or four different times, his salon crew walked out on him. Our city opened three new shops that year making the market too weak to handle the competition.)*

Tony's last-ditch effort was to pay for a refresher course to get my license reinstated so that I could take over and accommodate the clientele— the few that stayed. Desperate to regain some sense of who I was, I did not hesitate to say "yes" when he asked. It had been more than a year since I had an active cosmetology license. In order to reinstate it, I was required to take a refresher course at the beauty school.

Hard as he tried to recreate what was once a million-dollar salon, the shop stayed open for another year, and then folded like a paper fan. Before I left, Tony got me a position at a shop down the street and not far from home. The last day of Tony's shop being open, I packed up my curling iron and blow dryer and headed toward the shop known as Head Lines.

Linda was the owner of Head Lines and had left for the day. She willingly came back to the shop to let me in so I could set up my station. I knew she was coming from an event she was host for her Church and, when she pulled up in the parking lot, I got out of my car and said, "God answers prayer." In response she said, "He sure does!"

The previous year, I began attending a larger church that was feeding the spiritual needs of my children. They took on the physical needs of the whole family as well during our trials. Our church was well off and generous to its members. The couple in charge of the benevolence ministry was very understanding. They had similar experiences Bill and I were having, and if they judged, we didn't know it. Of course, it didn't hurt that I was trying to work off my debt to the King and cleaned the restrooms almost from the time we started attending. I also created and sewed all the costumes for Christmas plays made table covers, curtains, and anything else that would afford me a little "resolve." (I owed God everything and God meant church to me.) At one time, I sang in the choir, cleaned the bathrooms, the kitchen, helped with dinners, and was on the Board of the

Women's Ministry. I never said "no." As a side note, according to experts in psychology, our experiences in the past year and a half ranked top ten for creating stress. Compounded by my inability to say, "no," I created a situation that should have sent me over the edge. We were still emotionally intact, but physically the stress was taking its toll.

Bill stayed home and watched TV and complained about how much I was gone and the amount of time I spent at the church that was not bringing in any money. He looked for a job off and on, but a steady stream of rejection notices just created more stress. He was overqualified for most positions he applied for. Those positions he would have settled for were given to younger, less experienced applicants. Depression set in—for both of us. Both too consumed by our own pain to pay attention to the other's needs, we grew further apart.

Despite our financial circumstances, we were supposed to be okay, because the phone company retirement was received in a lump sum that we invested in long-term and short-term holdings. Instead, the money was dwindling due to doctor bills, car payments, and utilities. Don't forget the kids! We tapped into our short-term holdings, and then eventually into our long-term investments, losing more money due to penalties. Nothing was working out!

We believed the money we received and invested was supposed to serve us indefinitely while we would live off military pay! As I spiritually moved toward God, mentally I was screaming, "what are you doing? How much is enough to suffer because of bad choices? I thought you said I didn't owe you anything, that Jesus paid it all! What about the abundant life? This can't be what you mean, is it?" Then the reasoning of the Holy Spirit would comfort me with, "Lean not on your own understanding, but in all your ways acknowledge Him and He will direct your path." That was the only solace I was to receive from the Word for a long time. I didn't understand anything, and I was leaning on God.

When the jobs with the Army fell through, Bill tried to find other employment. He still had a few buddies in the military who helped him with a day of active duty here and there, but the debt seemed to compound faster than the income. A year later, the retirement money was running out and Bill still wasn't working when I ended up in the hospital. With each new year, I hoped this would be the one when redemption would visit us. Each new year I would say, "Maybe now!" Surely, God, we have been through enough! Somehow, someway I still hoped that God would redeem our situation and we could keep our home and Bill would believe that God loved us the way I told him.

CHAPTER 10

The Hospital

Off and on over the next year I was having belly pain. I went to the doctor, had blood tests, upper GI, lower GI, and everything in between without a diagnosis. Still the pain increased. Frequently, I suffered from head pain that would come in the middle of the night. The pain in my head and in my stomach would cause me to wake up. The pain in my stomach would become so intense I would vomit, feel better, and then return to bed without the stomachache, headache, or any indication why I would get either one. The only pain that didn't seem to go away was the belly pain. Finally, I was hurting so bad I could hardly walk. I took a lot of Tylenol, aspirin, and ibuprofen to relieve the pain so I could work.

Most people have a general medical doctor who makes referrals. After the referral is made, the specialist takes over. The only doctor I had seen in the past fifteen years was my gynecologist who knew me longer and better than any other doctor, so I continued to revert back to his care whether he wanted me to or not.

Four babies and years of female trauma had built a relationship of trust with him. Not knowing what else to do, and not being able to endure the pain any longer, I called my gynecologist. After a pelvic exam, he told me that my colon was inflamed, and I would have to have a colonoscopy. Great! I just started my job with Linda, and I was building a clientele. We didn't have insurance and couldn't afford the cost of medical attention and testing; what was I going to do with my clients? What about my kids? I couldn't take the pain anymore.

I bought the preparation and, for two days, lived off green jello, broth, and popsicles. The second day, I drank the first round of "Go Lightly"—the preparation that cleans the bowels from top to bottom. As soon as it started to act, I was on the toilet and heard a "POP." I didn't know what was happening, but this was the first time I felt relief from the pain in a very long time. I called my doctor who asked me a few questions and then told me to go to the hospital **immediately**! He told me he would call and tell the hospital I was on my way and they would have a bed waiting. He suspected what had happened and what I feared—my colon burst. However, there was no way I was going anywhere until I took a shower! After I took a shower, I would have to talk to my kids, who were concerned, because they overheard some of the conversation I had with the doctor.

I didn't realize the severity of the situation until later that night when I was told I had jeopardized my life by taking so long to get to the hospital. That shower could have cost me my life. As it was, it may have cost me my colon. After 12 hours, sepsis causes irreparable damage to the bowel, and up to 36 hours without medical attention, one usually dies.

The surgeon met me at the hospital and told me the possible consequences of this experience—none of which sounded appealing.

What he told me was I would stay in the hospital on intravenous antibiotics around the clock. Food would be withheld during that time in order for my intestines to calm down enough so that, during surgery, the doctor could determine if I would need a colostomy or only a resection. I really didn't understand a whole lot of what he was saying after the colostomy. It was the beginning of February and my hopes about this being a new year of redemption was fading. The place was all abuzz with nurses starting IV lines, asking questions, and calling doctors.

I heard myself telling the medical professionals that there was no way we could afford all this since my husband lost his job. So, do what you have to, but only the minimum. Their response was, "don't worry". Easy for them to say. In all the years of marriage, we had never been without the best medical insurance. Not once did I hear anyone tell me not to worry then. What I did hear was a lot of people asking a lot of questions about how the bill was to be paid. This was all so unfamiliar. I didn't know what to think or believe, but there seemed little I could do about it now.

The next morning, the surgeon came in first. He brought with him a floor nurse to do a procedure that would install a portal in my neck for dispensing all medications and nutrition directly into my carotid artery. The surgeon explained that intravenous lines are good for temporary use, but the veins collapse after a short time. In order to prevent the collapse, the IV lines are often moved from one vein to another. For my situation, due to the time I would need to be in the hospital, a portal that directly accessed the carotid artery was the best solution. So, the doctors (three by then) decided to do this life-threatening procedure to make it easier on everyone.

Only a surgeon is qualified to install the port due to the danger connected to possible trauma that would lead to bleeding. All this was done in my hospital bed with me laying on a downward slant in order to allow the artery to fill up and be tapped with ease. Thankfully, I had a good surgeon who knew what he was doing, and the procedure was a success.

Next, came the internist assigned to me to check my blood levels and chemistry during my stay at the hospital. Faithfully, the doctor I most relied on was my gyno. He would wait until all the others had come in, and then sum up their findings as it pertained to me with a reprimand and another "don't worry about the bill" speech, because getting well was "our" priority.

A week went by with the doctors checking on me daily. Not a morsel of food or a drop of water passed through my lips. All nutrition was received through the port in my neck, as well as two kinds of antibiotics eight times a day: heparin, to keep the port from clogging, and dyes that enhanced the CT scan, colonoscopy, and kidney function test. I received pain meds in my hips, but I often refused them since I was not having the pain I originally endured with an inflamed colon. (The only pain felt by the colon is due to inflammation, which causes swelling and creates pressure. When the pressure is released, the pain stops.)

I wish I could tell you that diverticulitis (as it was later diagnosed) was my only problem. Unfortunately, the CT scan revealed six kidney stones the size of quarters on all six lobes of my left kidney, a tumor the size of a grapefruit on my adrenal gland, which caused the headaches and vomiting, and endometriosis covering what was left of my female organs. It was decided that when the surgery was done, the priority was to take care of the colon that had ruptured and possibly remove the appendix, which had become a negative factor due to the surgeries I had prior to this hospitalization. Whatever else needed to be done would be determined during surgery. I continued to be at their mercy, as I already assured them that whatever they did, I couldn't pay for.

A wise woman once told me, if you don't attend church for any other reason, attend for the help that comes during a crisis, recognition of birth, a place to get married, and comfort during death. The church I had been attending showed me so much kindness. The wife of one of the board members came to the hospital to offer me several gowns to wear while recuperating, which I was not required to pay for or return. The Sunday school classes my children attended made cards for me. The women I had befriended during my stay at this new church took care of feeding my family and cleaning my house. My room was so full of flowers, we had to take them home periodically to make room for more. Never has anyone felt so loved as I did at this time. (Secretly, I "knew" it was a response to the time and energy I invested. That was okay; I had my own motives for doing what I did, and it got me noticed.) Besides the well wishes from Church people, my sisters made a show of affection also. It felt too good to be true.

The day of the surgery came. My pastor showed up to pray for me. Then I was wheeled to the holding area where everyone went before surgery. The woman at the "wheel" happened to be a member from the same church I attended. Coincidence? Not as far as I was concerned. She was very reassuring and also said a prayer for me before she had to leave.

After a little over four hours, the doctor exited surgery to tell my husband I had endured much, but the surgery was a success. He did not have to do a colostomy but was able to remove a section of colon and reconnect it. The tumor on my adrenal gland was removed, both of my ovaries and the mass of endometriosis that encased them, as well as my appendix. The doctor warned my husband that I was a very sick woman and not to be alarmed with what he saw after surgery. (We had that experience when my daughter had heart surgery. I hate when they say that. It made me feel like I was going to see a monster, or the remains of a person taken over by an alien. It gives me the "heebee jeebees".)

Well, I wasn't taken over by any alien, but I did have a number of tubes, pumps, monitors, and hoses coming out of every orifice except my ears. For two days, I slept while my body adjusted. Occasionally, I would hear a nurse or an aide changing my bags and checking my tubes. They would roll me from one side to the other so I wouldn't get pneumonia. When I finally started to wake up, I was hot—and not that kind of hot! I was sweating and couldn't stop. Someone turned up the heat.

I didn't know what was worse, the itch from the demyral I had been given during surgery, or the discomfort from the fire that burned somewhere inside. Finally, someone told me I was having hot flashes. I thought there was a beginning and an end to a flash. This couldn't be a hot flash. It didn't end. This was more like a hot marathon! Finally, I was given a fan. To everyone else, the room was as cold as a meat locker, but I was almost comfortable. One of my nurses suggested I ask about a hormone patch. The patch would replace some of the estrogen I lost when my ovaries were removed. It would also help to control my body temperature.

After two days, I began to regain some sense of what was going on. First the flame within, and then continuous interference to move me one way and then another. After a few days, there was a pain in my head that wouldn't go away. Nothing seemed to relieve it. When I started seeing the telephone making beautiful art on the wall as it rang, I figured something was wrong. The lights were too bright and taking on a different glow. I thought I was losing my mind! One of the nurses gave me a cold rag. Something had to be done about the nausea. I still had the nose tube in place and any nourishment I received was given through the portal in my neck.

First thing they did was change some of the antibiotics. Then ice packs were brought in for my head. I got a shot of Pepto Bismol in my nose tube. One thing after another was done, but without relief. I was starting to become agitated and vocal about not getting any relief. Finally, the doctor said if there was no reason they could find as to why I was feeling this way before surgery, then it must be related to something they were doing after surgery. Medical people are not stupid, but I was. They knew I was having side effects from the morphine, but were hesitant to remove it due to the amount of pain I would potentially be in without it. My body had gone through so much trauma, they were afraid that if they removed what was keeping me sedated and "comfortable," then my body would go into shock. There was also the matter of three drains that needed to be disconnected. (Sometimes I think if I had known what was involved in that, I would have endured the pain meds.) However, as soon as they disconnected that pump, I started to feel better. After the morphine wore off, my headache disappeared and I was beginning to feel like my old self, except with hoses, and pumps, and drains still connected.

The carotid pump was still being utilized to give me nourishment. The stomach pump was in place to remove the contents from my stomach before it moved into my intestines. It was all pretty gross. At one time, my sister and her daughter came to see me. They walked in and when they saw the drain that went through my nose and connected to my stomach, they left gagging. I think I would have done no less under the same circumstances. On the third day, I was asked if I could sit up, to which I quickly responded in the negative. I just prolonged the inevitable dizziness and weakness that nearly brought me to my knees along with the two aides that were helping to support me. Then, that evening, I was sitting up and dangling my feet off the side of the bed.

On the fourth day, the nurse came in to pull the first drain. To prepare me, she told me to hold my breath, and she would count to three, then pull. I thought she was just going to pull the drain that was used to keep fluid from building in my belly. When she counted to three, she pulled an eight-inch plastic tube that felt as though it was coming up from my leg. I didn't have to wait for her to tell me to release my breath, it came rushing out with a cry to God. Instant tears. All I could think of was that I still had two to go.

The morning of the fifth day, I met a new nurse who told me she would be pulling my second drain and was coming in to get acquainted and give me some pain meds, so I could be on top of the pain instead of trying to ease it after the fact. All I could think of was that I did this once and lived; I could do it again. The young woman didn't look old enough to entrust my health to, and certainly not my pain, but there seemed little

I could do. I took the pain meds and she assured me she would return in about half an hour. I have never been so close to God as I was at that moment. I would have been on my face if I could have gotten up. When the nurse returned, she gave me the same instructions as her counterpart: take a deep breath and, when she counted to three, she would pull. I did and she did. This time, I believe I cussed. Two down and one to go. I slept the rest of the day, worn out from the pain.

The next morning, I was seen by the surgeon, the internist, and the gyno—all pleased with my progress, all asking me if I had any questions. The only question that seemed pertinent to ask was if I could get a general anesthetic to remove the last drain. They laughed and told me I would be okay. Easy to say if you aren't the one on the other end of the drain.

The next day, the first nurse showed up. I had a little more confidence in her and prepared myself by holding my breath while she counted, one... two...three! Then, a steel cord ripped through my guts and took with it the rest of my organs—I was sure. I wanted to collapse, to pass out, anything not to feel the pain of this experience. At that moment, I couldn't believe my life had been spared to endure this torture. I glanced at the tube. Not only was it twice as long as the previous tubes, but tiny pieces of flesh were connected to it like the milkshake that clings to the straw pulled from the cup. This time, I was mad! I felt deceived and violated, a victim of my circumstances. There was nothing I could do. After about an hour, I was able to breathe normally again, so I called Bill to tell him the whole sordid story about what they had done to me. By this time, he must have been at his end, because he cried with me. That was a tender moment for us and worth the pain.

It had now been two weeks since I entered the hospital. The doctors were amazed by the rate at which I was recovering. One by one, the bags and the tubes were being removed. Each day, I felt stronger and stronger. By this time, I was able to get up and use the bathroom. The next week, I could walk and perhaps wash my hair. After the third week, they would see if I was able to hold the food in my stomach since I hadn't eaten in over two weeks now. After I ate, my bowels would have to function properly before I would be released. Everything was happening like clockwork, but I was anxious about going home. The attention I received in three weeks was more than I received in thirty years. I *felt* safe. I *felt* significant and unconditionally loved away from the world, isolated in my private room. I know now that it was a false sense of reality, but it was my reality. The only alternative was to go home to become a responsible parent who had a husband that no longer liked her and didn't have a job. I know why people don't want to get well and why illness becomes so powerful in the life of others. How sad to have nothing more to cling to, or gain attention from, than illness and pain.

The time for leaving was drawing closer. I made a last-ditch effort to remain and asked if the kidney guy could see me while I was already in the hospital. Anything was better than leaving the comfort of my womb—I mean my room. The only answer I got was that I was going to need a lot of time to recuperate from this experience, and then next year I could make an appointment with him. (It wasn't fair, God, to let me have all this attention and time where I could study Your Word and listen to worship songs, receive undivided attention from friends, family, and professionals, then drop me like a hot potato into the mess I left).

I was still sad when the young woman showed up to help me bathe and rub my back. Even though I could get up, staples, spoons and wires used to hold me together after surgery kept me from taking a shower and didn't allow me to maneuver very well. At about the time she was finishing, Bill happened to feel like visiting me. Another coincidence? Not in God!

As she worked, we made small talk; I asked how long she worked for the hospital. One question led to another and, by the time Bill showed up, the conversation turned personal with her telling Bill how to apply for a position at the hospital and where to go to check out availability. She even offered to take him to the Human Resource office. Bill returned an hour later with a job. Not the job of our dreams, but it held the hope for a better future. Was that a fast answer to prayer or what? It wasn't even a prayer as much as it was whining and worrying. But God...

Scripture says the Holy Spirit takes the groaning and uttering of our heart and turns them into petitions to God according to our need. He did it good! The next day, before I got out of the hospital, Bill was working. He came to see me on his lunch and assured me that there would be no problem taking me home when I was released. I hadn't seen him look this way in a long time. There was a bounce in his step, and he smiled once again with that signature smile. WOW!

CHAPTER 11

In the Meantime

Every evening, the first week after surgery, some of my family would come up to the hospital and spend time talking about their day and watching TV. Isaac would just lay next to me in the bed, satisfied to be there. Katie visited with Bill and Isaac once in a while, but she was old enough to stay home by herself and opted for that most of the time. Maggie hardly ever showed up because she "couldn't." Later, she told me that she could not look at me in the hospital bed, because it was too scary for her. Sarah came by once in a while, always with friends, and never stayed long. By this time, Billy was in college out of town.

Linda was very understanding while I was in the hospital. She even offered to call my clients and explain my circumstances. Every so often, she would call me to make sure I was doing well and didn't need anything. I voiced concern about the clientele I had built in the time I had been with her. There was such a short time from when I started at her shop until I went into the hospital, that I was afraid I would have no one left when I finally returned to work. She handled my dilemma with ease and, to my surprise, she and David purchased a huge Honey Baked Ham for us while I recuperated. I certainly didn't expect her to be so kind after knowing her such a short time. After all, I was an employee, not a friend.

I spent almost the whole month of February in the hospital. I spent another three months of recuperating at home before I was ready to get back to work. There was nothing that was not taken care of by the ladies from my church, Linda, and my family. Even the neighbors pitched in and offered their services. My daughter Maggie spent the whole month of February with her friend and their family who lived across the street. My three older children were able to care for themselves and took on the responsibility of Isaac when their father worked.

When I finally returned to work, understandably, there were a few women that found another shop. It was necessary to start building my client list again, but at least the pressure was off since Bill had returned to work. Everything seemed to be going well for a while. Time lost in the hospital and money lost when the military began its cutbacks put us farther behind. Although we were both back to work, Bill didn't make the kind of money we were used to, and I didn't have the strength to work any more than two days a week. We depended on our investments and our savings. When the money ran out, and we could no longer pay our bills, we were "forced" to file bankruptcy—again. This time, eliminating our debt and most of our material goods. How degrading!

The car that the State wanted us to sell, in order for us to qualify for food stamps, well...Repossession is a violating experience!

I just picked up the kids from school. While I was sitting in my living room, a tow truck pulled into our driveway, in the middle of the afternoon, and hooked up our van. I couldn't believe what I was seeing. I called my sister, who worked as a dispatcher for the police, to see what was happening. She had to tell me our vehicle was being repossessed. I couldn't even figure it out for myself.

Ouch! Ouch! Ouch!

This was the final straw! I always said that.

CHAPTER 12

Ministry Beginnings

While all this craziness was going on around me, Linda remained steadfast in calling and inquiring about my well-being. She is persistent if nothing else. Every day, she would call me at home if I wasn't working, whether she saw me earlier at the shop or not. Every day, she would ask, "What are you doing?" Every day, I would tell her, "nothing." The last thing in the world I wanted to do was become vulnerable to another human being. I couldn't trust God, why would I entrust my thoughts and actions to a "stranger." Besides, what I was doing most of the time was packing our belongings to go to who-knew-where, and that was not anything I wanted to reveal to my "boss." By that time, I was so beat down. I knew I wasn't doing anything of interest to anyone anyway. Besides, why would she ask? What did she want? I was suspicious, to say the least.

The only thing friends were good for, according to my experiences, was to hurt me. Keeping my distance and avoiding intimacy allowed me to survive what I knew; I was never going to be worthy of friendship. I didn't have time or energy for any of the pleasantries that go along with building a friendship, so I did what I did best when faced with difficulty: avoid and escape. I was never rude, but I was never available either. Well, that didn't deter Linda. That was okay, I figured I could wait her out. If I was to have a friendship ever again, it would be my way, on my terms, giving nothing. My life was about my thoughts, my pain, my past, my identity, and I wasn't willing to share them with anyone anymore! Eventually, she would get tired of asking and/or reveal her true self.

For two years, Linda called me. Eventually, my defenses wore down, and I began to soften. She didn't get tired, I softened. But I wasn't about to encourage her—not yet anyway. I still believed I must wait her out. Not once did I return her calls. It wasn't because I didn't want to, but now I was afraid to. Beginning to feel as though she might be sincere in her efforts, I became afraid that what I knew about me would cause her to shutter and run.

Once in a while, she would call and leave a message asking a specific question. Calling her back with an answer was a good enough reason to dial the phone. Otherwise, there was no way I would ever suppose that she wanted to hear anything I had to say. Calling without a purpose wasn't my style. There was a time when calling a friend was acceptable to pass time or stay informed, but that time had come and gone with the friends I previously had.

Linda had friends and, as far as I was concerned, I wasn't one of them, whether she thought so or not. I didn't belong in her circles, even though she continued to invite me in and around her friends. On some occasions, much to my surprise, she would introduce me as her friend. I wasn't worthy, and I knew it. It was just a matter of time before she figured it out. I wondered how long it was going to take. Two years of calling me without a return call gave me the courage to take a risk. One Sunday afternoon, when I got home from church, I called her for the first time without a valid reason. My fingers shook as I dialed her number. Thankfully, I got the answering machine and left a message. "Hi Linda. It's Shirley. Give me a call." Linda said she could hardly believe it and played the recording not once, but twice, just to make sure. Linda never acknowledged what I feared her finding out (abuse, bankruptcy, loss of home and vehicle, and so much more) but, almost four years later, I understood her persistence.

By then, we had unofficially begun Rapha Ministry , an emotional healing group for women, as well as started attending college. Oftentimes, we would walk after the group was over or before school started for us. More than once, I received revelation connected to our friendship, as well as God's investment in the details of my life. Walking made it easy to talk, as it was not necessary to look at Linda or have her look at me as we conversed about the deep things of God. The exchange of my "fig leaves" for His covering gave me hope for a new beginning and courage to put one foot in front of the other, leaning on and acknowledging Him.

CHAPTER 13

A Place to Call Home

A short time after I was released from the hospital and was well on the way to recovery, we received a foreclosure notice and a date to vacate our home—what was left of it. Usually, it takes about a year to complete the paperwork before you have to move. That gave me the time I needed to heal and begin a journey toward fulfilling God's potential—one that I couldn't have imagined then, but am living now.

We moved to my sister's basement. Carol's basement was previously owned by my mother. It was the house I grew up in. The basement wasn't a dungeon, but it wasn't finished either. Because there was not enough room, my girls were living with their older sister, who was renting an apartment with her friends. Sarah's friends were beginning to complain about her sisters living with them, because they weren't paying rent or food costs. It didn't seem to matter that they weren't eating there. It was the principle.

We didn't belong anywhere. Our family was split. My sister was gracious, but family and fish—after three days they both stink and need to leave. We stayed much longer than three days, but basement living was getting old, and I missed my kids. I didn't know what they were doing or how they were being treated. I didn't know if they were safe. What else could go wrong?

Not having any reason to believe we were going to be okay, except through faith, I asked my usual questions of God ... "Where are you God, and what are you doing?" I got the same answers as before, "Stand fast and know that I am God." Lean not on your own understanding... And, my favorite, His tender mercies are new every day. And I would tell myself, "Okay then, I guess we're going to make it through this disaster also!"

We were looking for a place to rent. It was difficult to go through the usual channels, considering our circumstances. Then, one of my friends from church told me her neighbor was selling his house. It had been on the market for a while, and she would ask him if he would be interested in letting us rent it until it was sold. Two months and two days later, we moved from my sister's basement to Fairview Heights.

All things are not what they appear. Actually, if I had walked through the house with my eyes "open," I might have seen some of what we later experienced. What I saw was a place where we could all be together; this was perfect! Really, I was grateful.

The layout was unique. The windows were every woman's dream. They were from floor to ceiling and looked out into a beautiful wooded area.

There was a wrap-around deck and a mother-in-law apartment attached. The original owner was a carpenter who added each additional space as he was inspired. Unfortunately, he failed to use the necessary tools to miter the connections and seal the floors. He was also not very good at finishing. Under the kitchen sink was a large hole that led to the crawl space. If you looked in the cabinet, you could see the dirt under the house. The cabinet in the bathroom looked finished until you opened the doors to discover the sideboard was missing and the 2x4s, that created the framework for the wall, were exposed. A beautiful stone fireplace captured your eye as you entered the living/family room. After a few days, we discovered there was a nest of pigeons in the chimney. It wasn't long before one of them fell to the floor, making a mess and lots of noise. That's where it stayed until Bill got home to get it out. That weekend, Bill put up some chicken wire to keep any more birds from doing the same.

At that time, Bill worked midnights at the hospital. One night, I woke up to the sound of the cats running and meowing, and then a "thump." I wasn't about to get up to see what they were doing. Whatever it was, it would have to wait until Bill got home. Meanwhile, I pulled the cover up tighter around my neck and tried to get some sleep. When Bill got home, I found out what was creating such a ruckus. Two mice had made the mistake of showing themselves to our cats. I now knew what was eating my toilet paper kept under the bathroom sink.

The house remained on the market while we lived there. After the first month, there were few buyers interested in the "zoo," so I began to think about decorating to make it feel a little more comfortable. I started to clean the windows and make some curtains. Then, I decided to rearrange Isaac's room. I could handle the mice since the cats were taking care of them and, unless it was nighttime, they stayed hidden under the kitchen and bathroom sinks. The birds were gone, but wasp nests were a different story. There hadn't been any reason to use the fan in Isaac's room, since we were at the end of summer and the weather was turning cooler. While I cleaned, I wanted some air moving. I got more than I bargained for. I got the air and the wasps moving.

Bill slept during the day until I woke him up with a blood-curdling scream, running out of the room and closing the door behind me. He promised to take care of it when he got up. There wasn't much more I wanted to do inside, so I decided to go outside and sit on the deck. I opened the door and, as if that wasn't enough, saw a little black snake sunning itself. Another scream. I didn't know where to go. Everywhere I went there was another species of animal or insect making itself comfortable in our space—MY space! If it wasn't a huge wood roach buzzing around the window, or crawling up the side of the couch, it was a spider the size of my hand on the door of the closet, or an alien cricket (camel back cricket is what I later heard they were called.) During the day, it wasn't too bad. At night, it was like all hell broke loose, and the cats had a ball (literally) as they would toss the mice and crickets back and forth between them.

When I told the owner of the home what was going on, he laughed and told me about the time he had to chase a big snake out of the hallway. (Okay, that didn't make me feel better.) It was probably a good thing we encountered so many mice and bugs or I would have had a difficult time leaving. I loved the layout, hated the loiterers. Loved the peace and tranquility but hated the woods.

We had almost three months there before it was sold. We quickly lost interest in buying it due to the wildlife that cohabited with us there. Winter was coming. Who knew what there would be to deal with. The closest I wanted to get to the great outdoors from here on out was looking at it through the windows of a well-insulated fortress, my car, or watching it on TV. I am a city girl. My idea of roughing it is to stay the night at a hotel that doesn't have room service or an indoor pool.

You can imagine how excited I was when another friend from church told us about a duplex in Belleville that just came open. Yea!!!!!!!!!! We talked to the landlord about our situation. He said whatever our circumstances were, he was willing to overlook that and rent to us as long as we maintained our end of the rental agreement. We stayed with him for eight years. Our whole family was together, and the location was close to everywhere we needed to go. Even if it wasn't, I would not have cared.

Sarah already graduated from high school a couple years before all the moves took place. Katie graduated high school the year after Sarah. Isaac graduated from Junior High School. Maggie got the worst of it when she started her Sophomore year at a new school. Fortunately, she already knew some girls from church that attended that school, but she would be attending as an outsider, nonetheless. Isaac would have the benefit of starting as a Freshman the year after we moved.

I can't count the number of times I asked God, Where? When? Why? But we were home, and maybe now we could begin to rebuild our family, our lives... our marriage.

CHAPTER 14

This Time For Sure

As time went on, we began to settle into a routine. The routine allowed us to relax. The more we relaxed, the more we began to heal. I remained in college during this time of trials and tribulation, although I did not remain with Linda doing hair. We didn't stop working together, but Linda sold the salon.

What is it about people trying to fix what isn't broken? About five months is all I lasted with the new owner—Joyous (No, didn't misspell it). That was her name, and she didn't mind telling you if you didn't enunciate it correctly. She would say, "My name is Joy-ous, not Joyce." She was a self-proclaimed alcoholic. Her mom and dad bought the salon hoping it would cause her to become responsible. Bad move...Enabling never works the way the enabler wants it to.

Joyous quit drinking for a while. But the more pressure her dad and mom put on her to succeed, the more suspicious and demanding she became of her employees.

Once in a while, I would go to the shop and visit Linda on my days off. Because I was in the shop, and sometimes helping Linda shampoo or painting my nails, Joyous assumed I was working and began asking me to pay for those days I was present. Needless to say, I didn't stay long after that. It became too tedious to explain myself over and over. Not long afterwards, Linda left, and then the rest of the girls. Joyous and her dad sold the shop—you won't believe who bought it! Remember Bonnie, the girl that I admired so much in my first job at Snooty Fox? She bought it. Her nail salon is upstairs and she lives downstairs to this day. She also rents a station to Yvonne who continues to do hair. I still don't know why that's significant but it seems to be, even now as I write about it. God knows; I'll leave it in His hands.

Linda got a job in a new salon. It wasn't long before she was calling me to come and work there too. I didn't think I necessarily wanted to work as a stylist, so I opted to become the receptionist—again. After about a year, I grew tired of reception work and started working Fridays doing hair. Not long after, I started on Wednesdays also. I just couldn't keep my hands out of hair. During this time, Linda and I were still pursuing a degree in psychology. I was pretty busy and loving it! I had new purpose!

Linda got me started going to college within two years after I started working with her in her salon. I really never anticipated going back to school after Cosmetology school. In reality, I was afraid. Linda was convincing and didn't mind going with me to show me around. That's what probably made the difference. Things began to turn around. Through each successful quarter, and then semester, my outlook improved as well as my self-esteem. I was becoming confident in my purpose.

At first, I began school with the intention of becoming an administrative assistant. That was my idea, not God's. After two years of struggling through those courses, I realized all the computer experience and typing skills were to prepare me for the next twelve years of internet searches and writing papers. There was no class I took that didn't require at least three papers. While I progressed through higher education in pursuit of a psychology degree, subject matter and research time increased. After twelve years, I succeeded in finishing college with a Bachelor of Arts degree majoring in Psychology and a minor in Religious Studies. Upon completion of the BA, I wasn't satisfied and continued until I received a Master of Arts in Psychology. Only God knew how that was accomplished! My children praised me for persisting, and my husband told me how proud of me he was! That made the last twelve years worth everything! I was the first of eleven children to get beyond the first year of college and obtain a bachelor's degree, much less a master's.

COLLEGE

Before I enrolled, I got lots of high fives and "you go girl" from friends, family, and coworkers. Some thought I was crazy. Everyone who had any higher learning told me I would do well, especially if I attended night school with the older students trying to better themselves. I was told the professors know what it's like to work and study, so they tend to be more lenient than the daytime staff. (Someone forgot to tell the professors.) I rarely had the experience of lenience. Evening classes took their toll and, I decided that if school was going to be this hard, I wanted to be awake so I could enjoy it. So, I enrolled in day classes.

After the first semester, I figured out that day school was easier for a lot of reasons. Younger people are way more forgiving and helpful than the older crowd. They were easier to talk to also, maybe because they didn't see me as the competition my peers considered me to be. Or, maybe they thought I was there to take up their slack. No matter, I found them to be fascinating and engaging for the most part.

Young people go to school because they are finding out what they want from life. Older people attend
because they found out that what they were doing is
what they didn't want or is what couldn't sustain them.
Along the way, the struggle to find themselves or be the
"best" took its toll. Many became hard-hearted. Those
that were still sensitive decided they didn't have time
to waste on amenities. Some had recently divorced.
Others had been relocated through the military. Two
people I came in contact with had lost their spouses
to cancer and the medical bills and lack of income required them to create some new skills and resources.
There were those like me, who decided that it was time
to step out of the comfort zone and try something new.
Most of them carried the weight of the world on their
shoulders. The lack of joy and peace was evident as they
set out to recreate themselves. **All** expressed concern
about the lack of time to complete the task. It made me
wonder and made me feel sad.

I was at least ten years, if not twenty years, older than
most of those who worried. Of course, I didn't have any
real urgency, nor did I have a definite goal revealed that
I was trying to achieve. Even if I did feel the urgency, it
isn't in my nature to worry anymore. Living in the "*If
Only's*" of the future robs you of precious time and energy in the present. I felt that I had all the time I needed
to complete the task at hand—still, without knowing

why. At first, I was just there for the grins. Later, I realized this process had a God purpose and was glad I wasn't aware of it before. Knowing me, going to school would have lost its appeal if I had considered it a job or an obligation. As the plan was revealed, so was the grace to process it emotionally and mentally. My spirit was guided by the Holy Spirit, and I reveled in the peace that surpasses understanding.

Living with the fear and worry of running out of time has created a generation of competitors that wore me out. When I finally made a decision to start taking classes during the day, I realized what a distraction it was for me to attend night classes surrounded by those in high-speed pursuit of their goals. While my peers had their schedules calculated until the day of graduation, my answer was that "I haven't figured it out yet." It was nothing for me to wait two weeks before classes began for me to register. While others ran around, waited in lines, and complained, I would wait for the rush and complete the registering process in less than a day— sometimes in a couple hours. Once in a while, I was influenced to fear as the others but would encounter one block and then another until I stopped. What turmoil!

Waiting until two weeks before the end of the semester was how I preferred to handle my schedule, even when I figured out why I was going to school and began to take it seriously. One time, I got confused with the dates and ended up registering the day before classes started. Everything always worked out, and I didn't spend my energy on the negatives. God is faithful! (You know, I only had to wait on a class one time in twelve years. As it turned out, there was a vacancy due to someone dropping out at the last minute, so I was able to register anyway.) Casting my cares and learning to trust God kept me from a high adrenaline level brought on by anxiety. Discovering what physical ailments resulted in worry was a lesson learned from my near-death experience two years prior to attending school. Take every day as it comes: "Take no thought for tomorrow, what you shall eat or what you shall wear..." At this time in my life, it was more appealing to enjoy the journey.

My investment yielded me a return in the form of good grades and greater confidence. Besides, I was having fun—finally. I was succeeding and discovering that I had an identity other than shame. School was not the only resource God used to reveal this truth. Linda and I had begun meeting with groups of women and studying God's plan for His children. Had I known the plan and how far I was going with my education, I may have maintained that high stress level I perceived in others. But, God...Who knows me better than I know myself, revealed as much as I could use to maintain a healthy confidence and peace. Timing was everything, and His is impeccable!

On May 13, 2009, I walked down the aisle to the platform for a handshake and a "job well done" from the President of Lindenwood University. After twelve years, I finished what I thought I never could start. My children and husband were very proud, and they whooped and hollered when I accepted my diploma for the Master of Arts Degree.

Because of the time, we were unable to go to dinner and continue the celebration. It was almost midnight. However, my children spent the night to continue the festivities the next day. We celebrated the whole weekend. The fruit of my labor was sweet.

Before graduation, I obtained a job in a minimum-security prison through one of my fellow students. I work for a contractual business that offers drug and alcohol treatment for those incarcerated as the results of drug manufacturing, selling, or use. My job function is to teach drug and alcohol recovery through behavior modification. This job doesn't necessarily require a psychology background but, from my perspective, we do a disservice to the those we counsel without it. As a matter of fact, all that is required is a high school diploma. The pay is an insult to my degree, but money has never been my motive for what I do. Don't get me wrong, I prefer to receive wages worth my time and investment but, in due time, I feel I will reap the harvest if I don't become weary and faint. There are always those who get paid more than what they have sacrificed to get. Life isn't fair. But God is, so I wait on Him to meet my needs. Then, there is the fruit of my labor that can't be measured in dollars and cents. Like the turn-around I witnessed in a 28 year old who had been in the prison system off and on for the last fifteen years. His reputation had preceded his introduction. I heard of him and his shenanigans the first day I began my new career. Silently, I prayed he would never be on my case load. God ignored that prayer.

What I learned about this young man ripped my heart. He was rightfully angry and untrusting of others, especially authority. At the age of eleven, his mother sent him and his sister to Florida to live with his dad. His dad didn't want them as they would interfere with his pursuit of drugs, alcohol, and risky living. His dad tried to contact their mom without results. She took off to Australia to meet the "man of her dreams" she had recently become acquainted with

through an internet connection. The young man and his sister got lost in the streets. In order to survive, the young man became a prostitute at the age of thirteen. He joined a gang for protection and was encouraged to use drugs.

In order to maintain his habit, he began selling the poison he used. He caught one drug case after another, ending up in juvenile detention. He fathered a son he was not privileged to welcome into the world, because his girlfriend found out she was pregnant after he caught the case he was serving time for presently. In an effort to control this man's behavior, he was diagnosed as being bipolar so he could be fed the medication that would subdue his rage.

After nearly losing him to another facility with greater security, due to his resistance to the rules of the program, it was a last-ditch effort to put him on my case load. This young man had God sense but was never discipled. He had limited knowledge of God's love and zero knowledge about why he was created. We started at the beginning where he got stuck in his emotional growth (age 11). Three months before he left, he began to refuse medication. Through the process of spiritual, emotional, and mental healing he matured, which created a satisfying and healthy outcome on his mind and body. Last week, this young man walked out the gates of Southwestern Illinois Correctional Center a free man—different from the angry, embittered little boy that entered the criminal justice system eight years ago.

CHAPTER 15

The Calling

Bible study was a huge part of Linda's past time. Not long after we were working together, she invited me to go with her to her weekly study. Naturally, I refused—but not for long. We met in the home of a lovely girl who welcomed me with open arms. It wasn't the first time I invested in a group that studied God's word, but it was the first time I really enjoyed a Bible study as a contributor. My usual experience was as a baby feeding from what milk I could digest. Sometimes, when I attended a study, I felt like an outsider. There were studies I attended with women that unknowingly confirmed my shame. I attended a study with women that were warm and generous who showed me what it meant to be humble—just ask them. There was a study at a church that always ended with women praying for each other. Oftentimes, the prayer turned into a time of "prophecy" which was nothing more than women speaking their convictions to other women about godly living. (I didn't stay with them very long.) The gifts of the Holy Spirit flowed freely in some and were suppressed in others. I learned something from them all, good and bad. Regardless of what I received, I always went away with the understanding that no matter how the Bible study is conducted, God shows up and redeems our humanness. His word never goes out and returns to Him empty but accomplishes what it was sent to do…because He is Love. Love never fails!

If you've ever participated in a Kay Arthur study, then you know that there is little left to the imagination. Many who study the Word need her style of teaching, because they are fearful to believe they could come up with their own conviction or they are lazy. One thing is for sure, her studies are absolutely thorough. There was a time when Linda wanted to conduct a study of her own using Kay's material and attended a few workshops (Kay Arthur strongly advises you to attend her workshops to present her work according to her style). Attending her workshops also made it easier to follow through with the depth of the teaching presented. I learned much from the workshop I attended but was not sold on the idea of teaching "her" material. On the other hand, Linda and her husband were teaching children's Bible study at their church and often searched for new ways to enlighten the young people left in their care.

Linda made friends wherever she went. With all the friends she had, she was never in want for anything to do. She was also known to spend a lot of time researching conferences and seminars on her own. Before you knew it, she had a van full of people taking a road trip to be a part of the results of her labor. On one such occasion, she attended a conference that changed her life.

Shortly after I began attending Bible study with Linda, she decided it was time for her to pursue a new direction, as she had an experience with God that filled her with sadness and motivated her to action. It was at this time, she received her calling to minister to the Christian woman who was bound by her emotional pain keeping her from living in the victory that Jesus won for her on the cross.

She had attended a conference with some of her church friends in one of the southern states. Although I didn't learn about her calling immediately after she returned, I knew that something was different. Later, she revealed she had a revelation while she was sitting in the conference listening to Jan Silvius talk about the fools in your life. Linda said, "I looked around the room and realized that every woman there was bound to their fool, unable to break free without help." Her heart was broken for them, and she knew that God was preparing her for something new. By the time she got home, she was fully invested in searching for the perfect study to begin the journey of healing for any woman that surrendered herself to the teaching of the Holy Spirit. She didn't know how it was going to unfold, but that never stopped her before! True to her nature, she just put one foot in front of the other, waiting for God to show up and show off.

Although I never presumed to share in Linda's gift of teaching, it was becoming clear as time went on that I, too, was being called. Actually, it was more like having one experience after another confirm what I had been thinking about for a long time before it manifested. At a very early age, I was in pursuit of purpose and emotional health. I was a good listener and a better giver of advice. Many times, the advice I gave was harsh and given without the benefit of the Holy Spirit's comfort. In my unyielded state, I was afraid to pursue a distinguished career. Without the knowledge and experience of grace, I believed it would be in my own efforts that I would succeed. I knew that was never going to happen, and the closest I would get to counseling someone would be while I tended to their hair.

There is a series of books by Dr. David Seamands that, although written in the '80s, still carries a fresh anointing. The books we chose were sold as a workbook or a reading book: *Healing for Damaged Emotions* and *Putting Away Childish Things*—two of the most remarkable revelations of God's intention and redemption for man that I have ever read besides Genesis. One book deals with the emotional trauma of life, and the other deals with the childish behaviors we develop to survive it. The wisdom contained in these books gave me hope, identified my true value, and defined my purpose in God. Through the years of presenting this material, I discovered who I was to God and who God was to me. It turned my world upside down by making the substance hoped for a reality.

Not knowing the process when we began, Linda presented, and I was there for support. Our first attempt at teaching this material began with the group of women we had already been meeting with for Bible study. After the first session, where we muddled our way through the book, we developed a strategy where we would tag team. It wasn't long before we developed a rhythm, by the grace of God, that allowed for the gifts of the Holy Spirit to flow and miracles of healing and deliverance take place right before our eyes.

Women were set free from anger that had come from as many different sources as there were women suffering from it. Most of them were stuck in the anger phase of grief due to the loss of a child, separation of parents, neglect, physical and verbal abuse, as well as sexual abuse. Anger is a peculiar emotion that is exemplified regularly by our care givers but rarely expressed correctly. We are told "don't feel that way," or we are encouraged to say what we feel at someone else's expense. Oftentimes, I hear that the expresser feels better after they unload their anger on the person they blame for their anger. In reality, they have expressed it, but they have also created more anger and/or more guilt suffered by both parties. Two wrongs never make a right. **If anger is stuffed, the result is devastating.** David Seamands said it is like trying to hold a beach ball under water. Sooner or later, your arms get tired and it comes up and pops you in the face. Sometimes, anger is medicated to help suppress it. Always when the angry person is taught how to manage and express their pain appropriately, it is diminished. The beach ball loses its air and resistance. If not, anger will be expressed one way or another—through sickness, pain, depression, mental illness....

Over the course of ten years, we saw God restore marriages. Women who attended these healing groups stopped blaming their husbands for failed marriages and began to take responsibility for the part they played in their relationship. Invariably, it was discovered that women lived the prophetic words in Genesis 3:16: "your desire will be for your husband and he will have rule over you." That scripture doesn't pertain to sexual desires like I originally believed. That scripture is better understood when you know that the desire God is talking about is the same desire that threatened to overtake Cain. The desire to control. Anger was crouching at the door of Cain to overtake him, but he was warned and graced by God to resist if he yielded to His Spirit. Our desire to control our husbands can also be resisted under the same circumstances. When the revelation of that scripture was received, the restoration process began.

One woman, I will never forget, had been holding a grudge against her husband for over twenty years. They were a military family stationed overseas at the time their baby daughter died. Their little girl became very ill while the husband was unavailable. They only had one vehicle, so she was forced to wait until her husband came home. By the time they got to the hospital, it was too late. This woman felt that her husband's absence was the cause of their loss. When she revealed the dynamics of her pain and forgave her husband, she was able to reduce the medication her Psychiatrist had been steadily increasing over the last twenty years to control her anger. Right before our eyes, we saw the veil of pain lift from her face, and she seemed to look younger when she left than when she came in. There was a smile on her face put there by God's grace, and she was able to complete the grieving process. Oftentimes, we would get good feedback from the husbands who were on the receiving end of these miracles. Sometimes, they desired their own emotional healing to be addressed.

Mothers forgave their daughters for not living up to their expectations. They now understood that the expectations to become what they weren't was unfair, and the expectations could never be met.

A granddaughter, robbed of her innocence by her grandfather, released the guilt of those experiences and surrendered to forgiveness. Some women forgave themselves for not being perfect. Other women carried the burden of "choice" that led to the murder of their unborn baby. You can't imagine the joy that comes when the burden of that guilt is surrendered at the foot of the cross. The grief of that experience haunts the individual daily as they wait for the feelings of forgiveness that never come. After accepting the responsibility of their choice, without justifying and rationalizing their circumstances, they are able to forgive themselves and once and for all times grieve their loss.

On more than one occasion we heard, "I know God forgives me, but I can't forgive myself!" Since when can the standard of a man be higher than the standard of the God that created him? It cannot be. Holding onto guilt keeps us from redemption and makes a mockery of the cross. Jesus is enough. Jesus on the cross is enough. As a matter of fact, his sacrifice was perfect! That's why God accepted it as a substitute for our sin and weaknesses. Isn't He wonderful!? Forgetting what was done to us, or by us, isn't necessary. We don't have to work for our redemption. The price was paid; the debt was cancelled! Pride keeps us from taking a hand extended to come to the foot of the cross and receive what has been freely given. Done! Isn't He wonderful!? We simply surrender our shame and guilt for His righteousness. We exchange our fig leaves for the robe of righteousness.

God graced us with a woman who came to our groups in a last-ditch effort to "restore the relationship between her and her sister that she felt was hopeless." (The reason for why we move towards God doesn't matter; He meets us where we are and restores us through Love.) After three meetings, she revealed to us that she was a lesbian. When first we discovered her circumstances, she was ready for us to reject her. Instead, we encouraged her to talk. At first, she argued that she must have been created this way because no one would choose a life that was so full of pain. By the end of the fifteen-week study, she became convinced that past trauma, bad examples, and choice led her to that lifestyle. She has since married her junior high school admirer who "found" her through the internet. He had been carrying a torch for her all these years. She and her sister were able to repair some of their relationship before her sister passed last year from cancer.

As we ministered to those in need, the anointing was strong. Words that were hidden in my heart encouraged, and exhorted, and comforted women of all ages, races, and religious affiliations. Scripture came alive and served God's daughters like I have never witnessed before. It seemed all we had to do was open our mouths and God spoke. It was like an out-of-body experience—standing on the outside of me watching and listening to me. Linda and I explained truth and revealed lies that we had no way of knowing except by the Holy Spirit. We would go into our groups with prayer. There was little we could study and prepare for except defining what scripture would be appropriate to use. Linda did most of the teaching aspect of the study. That never changed. The part I contributed was usually to create understanding about the scripture we used, and then personalize it according to what was being taught. Many nights, I would begin a group exhausted from the day's obligations. By the time the group ended, I was refreshed and energized.

Some days, Linda and I would walk. Over the course of seventeen years, I've probably put a million miles on these feet. Walking has always been a time when communicating with God has been the easiest for me, probably because I am busy doing "something" and actually doing "nothing." For a long while, before healing, it was the only way God was able to speak to me, since I spent so much time trying to work off my "debt" and hide from His holiness (which I was convinced would burn me up)!

As Linda and I walked, we talked, not shallow small talk, we dug right into the heart. It was no less than we did to those we ministered to. On one of these occasions, I began to talk about my heart-felt pain that continued to hold me captive and what I believed to be true about myself. I fought to dispel it without much success. I still believed I was created a vessel without honor and wondered how God could hold my wrongdoing against me when that was the way He created me. It was time to rip the scab off that lie.

I opened my mouth and began to reveal the ugliness of my confusion. Why did God create me without value? Why did He put me in a family He knew would abuse me? Why was I so insignificant? Why was I the only one who was unlovable? When would the debt be paid? What about my children? How could they survive and successfully overcome their beginning? Were they destined to settle for something less than what they desired: second best? As we walked, I talked. Linda said very little except to nod her head and reassure me she was listening. I was so mad at God, and yet I knew He was my only hope. I knew without Him and His resources, I was dead. Up to that point, seventeen years into my conversion, there were too many experiences that personally touched my life to deny Him.

We had come to the end of our walk and turned into the driveway of Linda's home. We walked into the house, not saying a word. I was exhausted. She offered me a drink of water and a place to sit. After settling in, I looked at her, and she replied, "God never intended you to experience anything but what He offered Adam and Eve in the garden. Just like in the garden, He will never overstep the boundaries of your free will or someone else's free will against you." There were more words of comfort that followed, but that was the most important part of the puzzle that began the process of exchange.

It seemed so simple. Yet, I knew that I was unable to comprehend it all these years until I had invested time and energy into discovering who God is and how He operates. Then, I got really mad! How could He let me live all this time without that revelation!? How could He allow me to believe so many harmful lies about Him, and me, and my family, and friends....

After I finished screaming at Him, I finally understood. Just in case what I believed was true, I spent most of my time hiding and running while adjusting and readjusting my fig leaves. Finally, after all those years, I was exhausted from running and ready to answer as He continued to ask me where I was, undaunted in His pursuit. Seventeen years after salvation, I was able to surrender all my bad choices and behaviors that allowed me to survive, and I was able to accept the shed blood of Jesus as my Redeemer, paid in full! The Holy Spirit was not yet finished. Whether we acknowledge Him or not, He continues to restore, to comfort, to encourage, and to care. It is impossible to come to the end of, or to deter, the unlimited Resource of Love.

CHAPTER 16

The Exchange

After reading that, some of you probably feel the same peace, and joy, and satisfaction, and love, and hope I felt. But the half has not yet been told.

We had been several years into the ministry by this time. We had done numerous Bible studies besides the healing groups. Unbeknownst to me, there was still a missing piece. There was still an area of my pain that had not been addressed. Deliverance was drawing near.

It was a series of events that took place this time. The walks continued. In an effort to help my family, and especially Bill, experience the same benefits of emotional healing I received, I threatened him with separation if he didn't agree to see a counselor. (If you can't get your way by being nice, then threaten is what I always said). Besides, I told him I would go with him.

After a while of seeing the therapist together, we began to make appointments individually. One particular time, I was in the therapist's office and he told me to close my eyes. I didn't realize what an effect this one exercise had on me. I knew I didn't like to close my eyes, but I always said it was because there are no secret agents in God's family, and there was no reason to be ashamed of any decision you make before God. I never believed there was any reason to close my eyes and do what I thought I could do with them open. Therefore, I always kept my eyes open.

None of these arguments would suffice for the counselor, and I closed my eyes. He began to ask me to picture myself as a little girl. Now, as an adult, allow the child Shirley to sit on my lap. Then he asked, "What is the one thing she would ask from you today?" That wasn't hard. I immediately replied, "safety!" Then, I opened my eyes and began to ramble about God, and who He was, and how He helped me, and the experiences I had with Him, and what I believed about Him, and how my faith would sustain me in this crisis with my husband. On and on I went until the end of the hour. As soon as time was up, I bolted out of that office as though I was shot from a cannon, making some excuse why I couldn't make an appointment. I told the therapist I would call later. I didn't intend to. I decided I was never going back.

What I failed to mention earlier was the circumstances surrounding this appointment. Due to the increase of clients, I was unable to get an earlier appointment, and my therapist was kind enough to stay over his usual departure time to see me. Unfortunately, staying after meant no one else would be in the office. We were alone. He was a man. I was vulnerable—still.

Safe in my car, I decided I would never return to his office again. There was no doubt in my mind what his intention was as I became vulnerable to him. What I failed to understand was that was my thinking, not his. All the fear and doubt I was experiencing was because of my own thinking. These circumstances, closing my eyes, being alone with a man, being vulnerable, were familiar to my subconscious mind, and I was making a connection between abuse and this moment in time with my therapist. My reaction to the present moment was fear. For me to feel some sense of safety, it was necessary for me to talk about God.

Although I said I would never return, I did. A friend who was retired from private practice, and a client of the salon where I worked, suggested I go back for the sake of the therapist, if not for myself. I made an appointment for the next week. It became obvious that my therapist had no clue what was going on in my head as I explained my revelation. He wondered why I had abruptly departed without making another appointment. And then, ever so gently, told me that he "would never knowingly hurt me." You know what? I believed him. That was my last appointment in that office. We mutually decided that my time with him had come to an end.

It was a good thing we ended with our respect and integrity intact. Some years later, he was my professor in the master's program, a mentor, and friend. I was so glad I did not lean on my understanding but acknowledged God to direct my path by listening to the advice of the other psychologist. This was the exchange of my facts for God's truth:

********A father and mother have a great responsibility to instill in a child's life: a sense of safety, significance, and unconditional love. These are God-given needs meant to be met by parents. When these needs go unmet, the child seeks to gain access to them by whatever means available. Many use drugs, some alcohol. Others use prostitution, debauchery, sexual deviance, cutting, and still others use financial success, material goods, living the "right" life with the "right" person, to substitute for these unmet needs that symbolize identity and love.*

As the child grows, they survive life by trying to control it. When they feel out of control, they draw from what is familiar to set up expectations about the situation, good or bad, in an effort to regain what was lost: either safety, significance, and unconditional love, or control. Most of the time, the individual is unaware of this process, and hardly ever does the other person know they are being played like an actor in 'scene one, act 2,700.' The only One who knows anything about this little drama is the One who can recreate it. His patience and long

suffering is unwavering, as He waits for you to understand.
****

I have never felt safe in my entire life! Because my father and mother didn't understand their responsibility toward me, I continued to look for safety, significance, and unconditional love wherever I could find it—usually misunderstood and a poor substitute. I didn't realize it but talking about God made me feel better. I read in His Word that Jesus stuck closer than a brother, that God's arm was not shortened on my behalf, and that times I am afraid, I can call His name and He will hear me and deliver me from all my fears. This was my way of proving Him without knowing if He would come through for me. That was the struggle or the battle I had to win; did I trust Him to be for me what I believed Him to be for everyone else? There was no doubt He was available for everyone else under the same circumstances, but I was never sure if I could trust Him. In the book of John 6:6, Jesus told us to prove Him, for He Himself knew what He would do. In Romans 12:2, God tells us not to be conformed to this world, but be transformed by the renewing of your mind, so that you may prove what is the good, and acceptable, and perfect will of God. Every experience where safety, significance, and unconditional love was an issue with me, I was proving Him without even knowing it. He was here, there, and everywhere in between. He never left me. He was always hoping, always expecting the best from me. He was pursuing me and waiting until I was ready to give up my old fig leaf for His covering. I know the angels rejoiced when I exchanged my shame identity for His robe of righteousness. I am still rejoicing!

Finally, I had a Father: God! Finally, I had a brother: Jesus! They consistently do and say what They promise, and I don't ever have to be afraid again! They are my purpose for being, and that makes me significant! The best of all, is that my behavior is not contingent on their love. They love me because God is Love! He will never operate outside the boundaries of His character, which is synonymous with love. That makes Him trustworthy—not because I believe it, but because it is true!

Bibliography

Allender, Dan, *The Wounded Heart*, Revised edition, Colorado Springs, Colorado, Nav   Press, 1995 (Page 49, 127).

Carniege, Dale, *How to Win Friends and Influence People*, Simon and Shuster, NY New   York, 1936.

Flemming, Victor, *Gone with the Wind*, 1940.

Harrison Harry, *Solient Green*, Adapted from: Make Room! Make Room! 1993.

Holy Bible, People' s Parallel Edition Copyright 1981, Tyndale House Publishers, Wheaton, Illinois 606187, all rights reserved.

Romans 8:1 KJV

Genesis 1,2,3

Seamands, David, *Healing for Damaged Emotions*, Colorado Springs, Colorado, SP Publications, Inc., 1992.

Endorsements

The life and ministry of Shirley Woods is a remarkable and unfolding story of faith, hope, and love. She is energized by the Holy Spirit with enthusiasm and giftedness to comfort and counsel others. I wholeheartedly commend her writings to you.

–Michael Van Britson
Pastor of The Father's House and longtime friend

Shirley takes us on a journey deep into hurt and pain but reveals how God heals the mind and restores our heart and soul. From start to finish, this read shows how our heavenly Father can pour out healing oil on our deepest wounds and transform us into a life of triumph and complete restoration in Him. In the end, we find that we are completely safe to fall into His arms of grace and know we are cared for and loved beyond measure!

–Ginger Johnson,
chemistry teacher and friend

CPSIA information can be obtained
at www.ICGtesting.com
Printed in the USA
BVHW061221290321
603630BV00009B/1068